Yankee Wake Up

Yankee Wake Up

Dr. Phil Maymin

CreateSpace Publishing

Scotts Valley, California

yankeewakeup.com
phil.maymin.com
phil@maymin.com

Publisher: CreateSpace Publishing
Scotts Valley, California, USA.

ISBN: 1438214162
ISBN-13: 9781438214160

These articles were originally published in the *Fairfield County Weekly*, online at fairfieldweekly.com.

The cover art is "Yankee Doodle" by Archibald M. Willard, circa 1876, commonly referred to as the "Spirit of '76." This public domain art is available on Wikimedia Commons and from the United States Library of Congress's Prints and Photographs Division under the digital ID cph.3b52205.

Printed in the United States of America.

Dedication and Acknowledgements

This book is dedicated to my family. The only reason I don't list each name is out of a libertarian sense of privacy.

I am also grateful to Tom Gogola. Tom is my editor at *Fairfield County Weekly* and it was at his suggestion that I began writing these articles right after the 2006 elections. Tom is an amazing person. He is not a strict libertarian in his policy beliefs, as you can see for example in "Shoot the Editor" on page 104, but, to me, his heart is a truly libertarian one. He is open-minded and courageous. In an alternative weekly, traditionally a very liberal and progressive space, he actively seeks out opposing points of view. He thrives on debate and dialogue. He allows the readers to come to their own conclusions without browbeating or censoring. And, like the true gentleman that he is, he always gives the other fellow the last word.

Table of Contents

INTRODUCTION

Who or what is a Yankee?

Ask an Australian or a European and they'll say it's an American. In America, a Southerner will say it's a Northerner and a Northerner will say it's a New Englander. In New England, they'll point you towards Connecticut. And in Connecticut? Yankees are probably in Fairfield County, the westernmost quarter of the state, the most populous, the richest, and the most free.

It's been that way for over 200 years. Even in the pre-Revolutionary period, it was a contemptuous term by foreigners for Americans generally, New Englanders in particular, and, most specifically, residents of Connecticut. Yankees were made fun of for being simpleminded. The song "Yankee Doodle," now Connecticut's proud state song, literally meant "American fool."

Why? Because a moral, principled person can appear simpleminded to those who waffle and hedge. And those unprincipled people, lacking logic and morality, can only scorn.

But it takes greater strength to declare "It is wrong" than to whimper "It depends." It takes a true Yankee heart to forge a nation where *all* are free, even the tired, wretched, and poor.

Are you a Yankee at heart? Read these essays and find out.

We Yankees founded a free and great country and promptly fell asleep for the next two centuries. But it is time to end our political hibernation. All is not well with the nation we made.

Yankee, wake up! America needs you again.

Phil Maymin, May 2008

Tuesday, March 20, marks the four-year anniversary of our invasion of Iraq. Why have we been there so long?

It's not because it's a global conflict: our involvements in both world wars were shorter. It's not because the conflict is so far away: it took less than three years to reach a cease-fire in the Korean War. It's not because autonomy and disputes about independence are so complex: even our own Civil War was over by now.

In one more month, the Iraq war will eclipse the First Barbary Wars of 1801-05 to become the second-longest war in American history, trailing only the 14-year Vietnam War.

Not the best of company.

And what have we achieved?

More Americans have died in Iraq than were killed on 9/11. Terrorists caused the deaths of 2,973 innocent people that day. Since invading Iraq on March 20, 2003, we have lost an additional 3,188 American lives, more than 95 percent of whom died *after* President George Bush announced the "end of major combat operations" on May 1, 2003.

That day, just six weeks after we invaded Iraq, Bush infamously boarded the USS *Abraham Lincoln* with a banner proclaiming Mission Accomplished. We had occupied Baghdad. Saddam Hussein had vanished and his reign was declared over. Hussein would be captured within six months. By all measures, we had won the war in Iraq.

Yet we stayed.

Bush's mistake wasn't that he was wrong in declaring victory four years ago; it's that he was right. We had won, and we should have left.

If we had declared victory and pulled out, the Iraq invasion would have been but a small blip in America's endless cycle of skirmishes, battles and wars. It would be grouped in with Afghanistan. Future history textbooks would gloss over it as retaliation for 9/11, just as they gloss over our Civil War as being about slavery. It would not be a big deal.

But because we stayed, it will become a big deal. Instead of Afghanistan, it will be lumped into a category with Vietnam. That's the best case.

The worst case is if people are still talking about the American-Iraq war 5,000 years from now.

Sound far-fetched?

There was *another* routine historical event in Iraq that happened 5,000 years ago that we still talk about today only because it took far longer than it should. That event? Noah and the flood.

The flood is most familiar to people through the book of Genesis, but essentially the same story is told in at least five other texts. In a recent book, Robert M. Best removes the mythical, embellished elements of the various stories to leave the legend of what probably happened.

Noah was quite likely a Sumerian king named Ziusudra who ruled Shuruppak, modern-day Fara, about halfway between Baghdad and Basra. A surprise thunderstorm in June, during Iraq's dry period, flooded the Euphrates River. Fortunately, Noah (Ziusudra) had recently loaded a commercial barge for transport down the river. When he saw the black clouds forming in the distance, he realized he and his family would never make it to the hills in time to escape the flood, so he loaded everything he could onto the boat.

While it took people by surprise, and indeed thousands of people likely perished, such a flood was not so uncommon as to be considered impossible. The valley experiences mild floods annually around March. The type of flood that Noah lived through was equivalent to the Mississippi flood of 1993 or the Saudi Arabian flood of 1985. Don't remember those two? If it weren't for Noah's mistake, you wouldn't remember the Shuruppak flood of 2900 BCE either.

Noah's flood lasted seven days. If Noah had simply landed then, his story would not be the most famous legend in the world. He would just be a lucky survivor.

Instead, Noah's ark apparently floated out into the Persian Gulf. Unfamiliar with the salty sea, and unable to see land anywhere, he and his family drifted around for a year.

And that unfortunate extension of time has made all the difference.

Have we fallen into the same trap as Noah? He floated 50 times longer than necessary because he got off course. Have we been in Iraq 50 times longer than necessary simply because we got off-course too?

We invaded Iraq for a variety of reasons: 1) to find and eliminate any weapons of mass destruction; 2) to topple Hussein; and 3) to prevent another 9/11. These reasons may not have been justified but they were the goals, or at least the excuses.

Each one was fulfilled within a few weeks of the invasion.

There were no modern weapons of mass destruction. Hussein went into hiding almost as fast as the Iraqi military leaders defected. We haven't had another 9/11 since 9/11.

It's not just unfortunate that we stayed there longer than necessary; it's fatal. If we had left when Bush had proclaimed the end of major combat operations, we would have had only several hundred casualties of war. Instead, according to the latest numbers from the Department of Defense released last week, 3,042 more Americans have died in "post combat ops," eclipsing the total lives lost on 9/11.

It should affect us strongly here in Fairfield County. After all, we were among the hardest hit on 9/11. Connecticut had the sixth-highest death toll of any state, and many of those were concentrated in our county. According to Wikipedia, Greenwich and New Canaan had more residents killed, as a percentage of total population, than any other Connecticut towns.

Noah remained at sea because he couldn't navigate his way home. He didn't have a choice. But we did. So why did we remain in Iraq? What were we hoping to accomplish?

The answer comes from Connecticut's history. We are known as the Constitution State because it was here that the world's first written constitution came into existence nearly 400 years ago. It was called the Fundamental Orders. It embodied the principle that government exists to protect individual rights and that government is limited in its powers. The individual rights spelled out in the Fundamental Orders are still part of our current Connecticut constitution, adopted in 1965. They are included as the Declaration of Rights in the very first article.

We stayed in Iraq to help them write a constitution.

Had the Iraqi constitution invested wholly in the Connecticut and American principle of individual rights and limited government, many problems would likely have quickly disappeared. The oil and gas would have been sold to the highest bidder and become a private concern. Taxes would likely have been completely unnecessary given the huge financial windfall. Courts would have been established to adjudicate contract, tort and criminal matters. Iraq could well have become the freest, richest and most prosperous country in the region.

We went the other way. Unlike Noah, we had a choice, but we chose wrong.

We gave Iraq the exact opposite constitution, one of unlimited government without regard for individual rights. One of the principal authors of the Iraqi constitution was Hamid Majid Mousa, former Secretary of the Iraqi Communist Party. He is now an elected official on the Iraqi National Assembly.

The Iraqi constitution essentially mirrors the Communist Party USA platform. Both guarantee the right to a job and to a living wage. Both guarantee decent housing. Both guarantee unlimited health care. Both guarantee unlimited education.

Communism doesn't work. Those who are able, work less, and those who are not, demand more, until rationing sets in. Ukraine used to be known as the "bread basket of Europe" because its fields produced so much bread, but once it fell behind the Iron Curtain, not once in the 70 years of Soviet rule did Ukraine produce enough to even feed its own people.

Now the oil and gas of Iraq is owned by "the people," to be managed by the central government, with proceeds distributed to the various regions based on need. The ghosts of Marx and Lenin have descended on Baghdad. Is it any surprise that Iraq is no longer able to generate enough oil and gas for its own people? Eventually, there will be fraud and abuse because the Iraqi government will be in a position to hand out oil contracts to foreign companies. But is generating revenue for American companies a military matter? Is it worth the lives and the money?

When Noah and his ark finally came ashore after sending out doves and crows to test for land, they knew immediately they were in trouble. They had been the custodians of the assets on the ark, and they had eaten them all. Noah knew that when people back home learned the ark had not been destroyed in the flood a year earlier, but had merely been floating around, there would be plenty of debt-collectors looking for compensation for their missing wares. Indeed, Noah and his family faced bankruptcy, slavery and a miserable life.

Their solution was to cut and run. They sold their remaining assets to a local temple in order to receive religious protection. Noah was granted an office similar to a modern-day justice of the peace. They then separated and lived out their lives far away from home.

That's the problem with staying in Iraq indefinitely. It will result in a desperate cut and run later, instead of an orderly withdrawal through strength today.

If only one American war is remembered 5,000 years from now, it will not be Vietnam, because there was never a time when we could have left Vietnam victoriously. That was simply a drawn-out defeat. Iraq is shaping up to be a defeat snatched from the jaws of victory.

And if the defeat results in a desperate America seeking protection from its growing list of creditors, that is the sort of thing people will remember through time.

The tale of Noah concludes with heavenly laws passed to Noah, the so-called Seven Noahide Laws, commemorated by a beautiful rainbow. These are the laws that a society must follow to be considered righteous, and they predate the Ten Commandments by more than a thousand years. They are essentially libertarian laws that formed the basis for our belief in individual rights and limited government.

Six of the laws tell us what to refrain from doing—murder, theft, adultery, idolatry, blasphemy and animal cruelty. The seventh tells us what to actually do. It tells us to have laws that are just. To set up courts to adjudicate disputes. To enforce the preceding six laws. In short, to be libertarian.

All we needed to do in Iraq was set up a Noahide Constitution, and we failed. Can there be anything more ironic than that?

Well, there is one thing. The Seven Noahide Laws are actually mentioned in American federal law. Public law 102-14 established Education Day and stated: "the historical tradition of ethical values and principles which are the basis of civilized society and upon which our great Nation was founded...have been the bedrock of society from the dawn of civilization, when they were known as the Seven Noahide Laws."

This law was passed exactly 12 years to the day before we invaded Iraq, and exactly 16 years ago this Tuesday. And it was signed by President George H. W. Bush.

It's not too late to get out of Iraq. There is a way to do it safely and while maximizing America's national security interest. The only question is if we are ready, like Noah, to eat crow.

Originally published on March 15, 2007

In the past month, we've both eaten turkeys and voted them out of office—but the roots between Thanksgiving, politics, war, and the Nutmeg State go deeper than that.

Connecticut is known as the Constitution State because it was the home of the first written constitution in the history of the world, but it could also equally well be called the Thanksgiving State because it was the home of the first adoption of an annual day of general thanksgiving.

The funny thing is, both happened in the same year.

What was so special about 1639? We had just defeated the Pequot Indians, whose name translates either as "the destroyers" or "a shallow body of water." No one knows for sure. (In 350 years, how will "al Qaeda" be translated?) The war was fought over our ability to trade fur freely, or at least that's what I wish it were about. There had been violence from both sides and one attack in particular, their version of our 9/11, was blamed on the Pequots, though apparently another tribe altogether was responsible.

Nevertheless, we fought the Pequots and essentially wiped them out. We won the war in 1637.

Note that September, 1637 was not "the end of major combat operations" but the end of the war.

We won.

It was over.

The next year, Connecticut started forming a government. It took several months to write a constitution, called the Fundamental Orders. It was a document that would later serve as a template for the American constitution, and one whose text is still included as Article 1 in the current Connecticut constitution, adopted in 1965, as the "Declaration of Rights."

They knew what they were doing in deciding to write down how they wished to be governed. It kept those in charge from changing the rules of the game. It secured freedoms.

The constitution was adopted January 14, 1639, and eight months later, on September 18, 1639, Connecticut proclaimed the adoption of an annual day of general thanksgiving.

Peace bore fruit.

Peace meant feasts.

What's going on with Iraq? If we won the war, why are we still fighting? What does it mean to have won if we won't be governing the province as a territory but giving it back to the same people we took it from? What if the Iraqis elect basically the same government we overthrew? Do we have to come back?

If our military took its cues from our Connecticut forefathers, we would have won the war in Iraq convincingly. We would have established a constitution for the region, whose primary aim is protecting property rights. And the resulting freedom would have been celebrated with a feast for all.

Could the constitution been written correctly? Sure. A constitution is not hard to write when you have such excellent models as the American version. But the Iraqis, guided by the Americans, chose a different direction. They chose to essentially copy the Communist platform.

What a mistake. The Iraqi constitution guarantees employment at a decent wage for every citizen of Iraq. It guarantees education "at all levels," presumably including everything from a videotape of Sesame Street to a particle accelerator. The Iraqi constitution guarantees housing, health care, retirement and disability benefits, and everything else you could imagine. The oil is owned by all Iraqis, managed by the central government, and its profits distributed to the various ethnicities based, quite literally, on "need."

Could we have afforded a monstrous feast?

Sure.

We've spent much more than $300 billion on the war. There are about 30 million Iraqis. That's $10,000 for every Iraqi man, woman, and child. A few years ago, before we devastated their economy, the median income in Iraq was about $250 per year. That means half the people earned less. Instead of the war, we could have paid every Iraqi the equivalent of 40 years of salary.

If we had just taken a cue from our Connecticut forefathers, we would have won the war, created a proper constitution, and celebrated with an annual feast for many centuries.

We continue to celebrate, in freedom, our annual Thanksgiving here in the Constitution State. We've just done so. We could have given the same gift to Iraq. Instead we've established the next Soviet Union. The Iraqis won't be able to feed themselves or pump enough oil until their constitution is rewritten, because Communism doesn't work.

We didn't learn from the success of our Connecticut forefathers, and so it may be another century before there is a feast in Iraq.

Originally published on November 30, 2006

"SWIPER NO SWIPING!" DORA THE SOCIALIST EXPLORER?

The children's television show *Dora the Explorer* has generated billions in revenue from retail sales alone and has captured the imagination of children everywhere. On the surface it's a quasi-interactive bilingual show about the misadventures of a young girl and Boots, her companion monkey, but according to a list of trivia on Wikipedia, it was also the first show to begin a trend of "applying liberal politics to children's shows."

Is Dora a subversive attempt to mold more Democrats? Perhaps it's a subtler version of *Why Mommy is a Democrat*, which illustrates such stereotypical socialist mores as "Democrats make sure we all share our toys, just like Mommy does." From what I've been able to gather, even many Democrats cringe at the book's depiction of their party as totalitarian apologists. Surely the party whose ideal is social libertarianism can offer more progressive ideas than tax-and-spend, just as the Republican Party whose ideal is economic libertarianism can offer more conservative ideas than tax-and-war.

I have watched my share of *Dora*, and what's most interesting to me is a minor character named Swiper. I'm not alone in my fascination: the same Wikipedia article devotes more than a thousand words to Swiper; Dora gets less than 150.

Why is Swiper so interesting? I think the creators of the show, perhaps unconsciously, made the character the embodiment of government. And viewers, sensing that familiarity, perhaps also unconsciously, trigger in themselves the same feelings of unease that they get when thinking about government itself.

Like the government, Swiper the Fox appears in every episode and tries to steal an important item from Dora. Yet Swiper doesn't need or use the item himself. Instead he merely hides it and Dora finds it again. He will apparently also return the item if the right lobby group comes calling: Swiper has an affinity for puppies; when Dora says an item is a present for her puppy, Swiper hands it back immediately.

Swiper is clever, a technical wizard—like a savvier Coyote from the *Road Runner* cartoons. He wears disguises and sneaks around a lot. He nearly always appears in a blue mask and gloves. Government, too, is largely anonymous, and has impressive domestic espionage abilities.

Swiper the Fox has his counterparts in other lands: the French Fifi the Skunk, the Tanzanian Sami the Hyena, the Russian Fomkah the Bear, and the Chinese Ying Yang the Weasel. Every country has a large portion of its government that does nothing more than redistribute. It takes important items from you and hides them behind a load of paperwork, bureaucracy, and cronyism. Whoever finds it (or, whichever special interest claims it), gets it. Sometimes, as with Dora, it is even the same person from whom it was taken in the first place. In all cases, it is not Swiper or Fifi or Fomkah who use the object themselves. Were that the case, they wouldn't remind us of government but of thieves.

But don't we need someone in charge who makes sure our wealth gets distributed fairly? The question answers itself. Whoever is in charge of distribution is essentially the owner. I can distribute only what I own. I can't distribute your property to others any more than you can distribute mine. It's like the caricatured Democrats above who "make sure we all share our toys." By implication, the Democrats own all the toys and there's only one way they could have gotten them: by swiping.

Fortunately, there is a way to stop Swiper, and it is the ultimate clamp on government, too. Before Swiper appears, a menacing whisking sound reverberates in the background. If you help Dora spot Swiper in time, you just have to yell "Swiper, no swiping!" three times. She usually succeeds, causing the frustrated Swiper to snap his fingers and mutter, "Oh, maaaann!"

The whisking sound in the distance is getting closer every day. How many items have we lost to the fox? How many times have we been fooled when the fox disguises himself as a donkey or an elephant?

There's only one way to stop it.

We have to yell real loud.

Originally published on August 23, 2007

This week, Congress begins its "lame duck" session before the new Democratic majority takes over in January. Where does the term "lame duck" come from? And what does it mean for Fairfield County?

To us moderns raised on a steady diet of Seinfeld reruns, "high-finance" means bulls, bears, and people from Connecticut. Three hundred years ago in London, there was a third animal, as high-finance meant bulls, bears and lame ducks. Back then, there was no central area designated as a stock exchange, so brokers gathered in coffee shops on Exchange Alley to trade their holdings. The Starbucks of the era was Jonathan's Coffee House. When it came time to settle up, which the brokers did once every three months, there was often the problem of the broker, or his client, who didn't have the cash. What to do with such blaggards? Civilized Londoners banned them from Jonathan's, though they were still allowed to act as brokers, in their own offices. We can only infer that the manner in which such lame ducks waddled out of the coffee shop inspired the nickname.

The term would eventually come to apply to voted-out politicians going through the motions in their last days of power. These politicians had been banned from the metaphorical coffee shop of elected office, and spent their last moments waddling. A lame duck can still quack angrily, but can't do much about it.

Expect a lot of angry quacking this month, even if Fairfield County doesn't have any lame-duck representation at the federal level. We managed to keep our incumbents in both the Senate (Joe Lieberman) and the House of Representatives (Chris Shays), even though the former lost own party's primary and the latter was a strong supporter of the war in Iraq in an election when Democrats rolled to power on that issue.

The term "lame duck" has been narrowly, and perhaps unfairly, applied to these particular politicians. A lame duck is a person who reneges on his promises, whether he was voted out of office for it or not. If an honorable politician kept his word but was voted out anyway, no self-respecting Jonathan's coffee drinker would have considered him a lame duck. A lame-duck politician is any politician who breaks his contractual oath. Brokers and politicians promise high gains with no downside, but they aren't banned until they fail to deliver. For a broker, it is the cash to buy the security. But what is it for a politician?

The most important promise every politician takes is an oath to uphold the Constitution. They pledge to put personal feelings aside on any issue if it violates the Constitution. They may not like terrorists having free speech or the right to due process, but they must uphold the Constitution. On the issue of gun ownership, they may not regulate it, restrict it, or infringe on it in any way. Yet virtually all of them do. And we let them get away with it.

We could take a lesson from those British coffee drinkers of three centuries ago. They tried banning bad people, like we tried voting them out of office. Nothing changed, either for them or for us. For every banned politician or broker, another unscrupulous one would take his place.

The Democrats won't get us out of Iraq any sooner. Taxes and spending will go up. Our freedoms will keep getting eroded.

What did those brokers do? They bought a nearby building and called it New Jonathan's, later renamed "the Stock Exchange," and they began levying fines for violations. The political equivalent would be secession—but we don't have that option. A portion of our country once tried to make a new America, and the result was the Civil War.

So what can we do? There's no easy answer. We can only hope to vote better next time.

Ultimately we should look up for eagles, not down for ducks, for our candidates. Eagles are the symbol of our country and our Constitution. Eagles soar. Eagles are beautiful. If we ignore them, they'll become endangered, and eventually disappear. And all we'll be left with is a bunch of quacks in Washington.

Originally published on December 7, 2006

WHO ARE YOU CALLING A TURKEY?

Nowadays people think a declaration of independence needs to be followed immediately by a constitution. But our founding fathers had other priorities. On that same fateful day of July 4, 1776, the Journals of the Continental Congress reveal what was most pressing. "Resolved," it declared, "that Dr. Franklin, Mr. J. Adams, and Mr. Jefferson, be a committee, to bring in a device for a seal for the United States of America." First and foremost, we needed a corporate logo.

According to the excellent historical site greatseal.com, it took six weeks, but finally each committee member brought in a suggestion. Franklin suggested a picture of Moses standing on the shore, bathed in a divine light on the shore, with his hand raised over the sea and waves crashing on the Pharaoh.

Jefferson suggested a picture just a little later in the same Biblical narrative, of the Israelites wandering the wilderness, following a cloud by day and a pillar of fire by night.

Adams wanted a picture of Hercules at a fork in the road, choosing between self-indulgence and honor.

Can you imagine any of these seals on a podium fronting George Bush? Neither could the Continental Congress. It was back to the drawing board.

Over the next six years, two more preliminary committees submitted ideas such as a warrior holding a sword and an olive branch, a "phoenix in flames," a pyramid with a floating eye above it, and a rooster.

Finally, as peace talks were underway in Paris in 1782, a deadline was upon us to come up with something that could be used to properly ratify a treaty. If you've ever had to order business cards for a new business in time for a particular event, you know the pressure they felt of coming up with a logo basically overnight.

So we got the bald eagle. A couple years later Franklin expressed his disappointment. The eagle, he wrote, was a cowardly bird, and of bad moral character. What he wrote was essentially a poetic description of the government we have today. "Too lazy to fish for himself, he watches the Labour of the Fishing Hawk; and when that diligent Bird has at length taken a Fish, and is bearing it to his Nest for the Support of his Mate and young Ones, the Bald Eagle pursues him and takes it from him."

Franklin would have preferred a turkey. The turkey is the only poultry native to America. And it is, "though a little vain & silly, a Bird of Courage, and would not hesitate to attack a Grenadier of the British Guards who should presume to invade his Farm Yard with a red Coat on."

In the two centuries since then, we have learned even more about turkeys that would have made them a better choice. They have been around for more than ten million years. They can spot movement on from one hundred yards away. They can be heard from a mile away.

If we as citizens could only have spotted the big-government movement that has been happening over the past hundred years, or if we could only have made enough sound to have been heard, perhaps we would still have all of our liberties. We no longer even hesitate, let alone actually defend our homes from an attack. We hand over our most private information voluntarily, and do not object when it is taken from us by stealth, because we are not terrorists. We have nothing to hide. Let them brand us and track us and videotape us.

Instead, we have become even lower than the eagle that presides over us. We have been tamed, and that's the saddest thing of all. Wild turkeys can run up to 25 miles per hour. Wild turkeys can fly at up to 55 miles per hour.

But not domesticated turkeys. They and we merely eat, reproduce, and wait to die.

Isn't it time we stopped letting our government give us the bird?

Originally published on November 22, 2007

The word "environment" gets people heated and passionate, especially in wealthy suburban areas like Fairfield County. Pseudoscience battles science, emotions battle logic, and government battles freedom, sometimes within the same person. No one wants to destroy Earth for future humans, but no one wants to make current humans suffer either.

In addition, there are too many factual claims and counterclaims to keep track of. Let's instead try to tackle the issue from a purely logical perspective. When it comes to the environment, the real issue is pollution, or damage to the environment caused by humans. It can be split into four different kinds:

1. **A few polluters and a few victims**: Suppose someone dumps their garbage on your lawn. The remedies are straightforward: They can be held liable to you for money damages, and can be arrested for criminal trespass. Injunctions and other remedies are also available to prevent future infractions. There is no need for any legislative government action whatsoever, any more than we need new laws against murder or theft. Murder by pollution is still murder and doesn't require a separate statute.

2. **A few polluters and many victims**: Suppose someone poisons a town's reservoir. Money damages for the citizens would be hard to calculate and distribute; that's what class actions are for. But the real legal teeth come from the criminal penalties, as harsh and stiff as they would be for anybody who caused so much harm to so many civilians. No need for any legislative action—we need *less* legislative action: The antiterrorism laws

Congress has been passing are stripping everyone of the liberties government is supposed to protect, and the very liberties that lead the free market to inexorably decrease pollution over time, as it has always done.

3. **Many polluters and a few victims**: Suppose you are among a few people who live next to a busy highway and you have to breathe the smog from thousands of cars a day. It's not at all clear how to identify who to sue and how to partition the damages among them. The police are powerless to track down every car that has ever raced by your home. The only solution is to sue the owner of the highway (the government), for damages. If the highway were privately owned, you could sue the company and it would pass the increased costs on to the drivers, who could either pay the higher price, drive different cars, or carpool. The only difficulties come about when government is doing the polluting, because in many cases, government can refuse to let you sue them. And indeed, the American government is the largest polluter on Earth.

4. **Many polluters and many victims**: Suppose third-world nations are polluting the Earth, and there are too many companies and countries involved. Americans, current and future, are suffering. What to do? There is no court with the jurisdiction and not enough of a police force to stop everybody. This, finally, is the only and proper role of legislative government: defend our borders. If foreign countries are invading our borders with poisons, intentionally or not, that's what our government exists to protect us from. We can argue or vote about different strategies for dealing with them. Bombing or invading polluters will cause severe backlash and wars. Paying them off is likely to encourage other polluters hoping for a reward, the way countries like North Korea are encouraged to pursue nuclear weapons in the hopes of an American payoff. The easiest solution might be to negotiate sufficient payment from them to us to cover our

costs and damages. It is a difficult number to calculate honestly and a hard one to enforce as well, but at least it puts us in the moral high ground: We are protecting ourselves.

In three out of the four cases, Congress should do *nothing* because it is a judicial question. In the last case, Congress negotiates with foreign governments and defends our borders, but it does not restrict in any way the rights of Americans.

Isn't it funny how different that is from the common environmentalist approach of assuming that you are to blame, that your behavior is the one that must be modified, that we need Congress to pass lots of new laws controlling your life?

Does it sound paradoxical that the best way to protect the environment is to have fewer laws? It's not. It's simply logic.

Originally published on June 7, 2007

Connecticut's Department of Children and Families (DCF) can seek custody of your children for "educational neglect," a charge typically levied against homeschooling parents. But can educational neglect even be defined in a way that applies only to homeschooled students, excluding both publicly and privately schooled children?

Suppose a child hasn't been adequately taught how to read and write. Is that educational neglect? Sixteen percent of all adults in Connecticut—more than half a million people—are functional illiterates, according to a 2001 municipal report for the town of Hartford. Meanwhile, Joseph Heranes, a home-schooled 14-year-old from Avon, just tied for third place in the national spelling bee. How many public school students can spell punaise, furfuraceous, or triticale? How many private school students?

Suppose a child hasn't been taught astronomy or chemistry or biology or creative writing. Any of those assumptions apply equally well to a large fraction of public and private school students. Should they be taken away from their parents for educational neglect as well?

Clearly the definition of educational neglect cannot include the failure to learn or be adequately taught any subject matter that is also taught in public or private schools, because there would be plenty of failing school-attending students who would be subject to such a definition, too. And definitions that touch on religious subjects, such as creationism vs. evolution, are properly prohibited by the separation of church and state.

Could an explicit exception be made for publicly or privately schooled children? Define educational neglect as, for example, illiteracy, but make parents who send their children to public or approved private schools exempt from the charge because it is the fault of the teachers, not the parents.

Such an exception would be patently absurd. It's like exempting the people who hire mercenaries from murder, or the board of directors from fraud committed by their chosen CEO, on the theory that if you hire someone, you're no longer responsible.

Parents, not the government, are responsible for their children. If they choose to outsource certain aspects in order to benefit from the free market, whether it's traditional education, karate, or music classes, the responsibility is still theirs. Finally, if an exemption for public and approved private schools is built into the very definition of educational neglect, then homeschooling becomes essentially illegal. And Connecticut has no right to pass such a law. Even the threat of persecution by the DCF sends a chill down the spine of anyone who sees parents hiding their homeschooled children during daylight hours so truancy officers or DCF agents don't demand entry into their home.

Indeed, the whole concept of mandatory schooling is, if you take a broad perspective, quite shocking. The Connecticut Constitution ensures "free public elementary and secondary schools in the state," but nowhere does it state that education is compulsory. That law is Conn. Gen. Stat. 10-184. And what should be done with truants? Conn. Gen. Stat. 10-200 elucidates: "The police... shall arrest all such children." Are these laws even constitutional?

Mandatory education is even worse than a sentence of forced community service. It's more like school arrest. All children between the ages of 5 and 18 must spend six hours every weekday, nine months out of the year, in a brick building with other inmates, where they must sit when told to sit, eat when allowed, and walk in slow circles catching only brief glimpses of the sun and the earth during periods called recess. They are allowed home for dinner and bed but they must do additional work even at home or face disciplinary action. The few who escape are caught by truancy officers and forced back in. Repeat offenders go to juvenile detention. The forced attendance has the same effects in schools as in jails: boredom, recidivism, sex, and drugs. Probably the only places in America that have more illegal drugs than prisons are schools.

What have all these children done to be punished this way? Their only common factor is age. Since when do we punish people for being a particular age? Even a sentence of forced community service requires a trial. When was the trial held that hammered down more than a decade of school arrest on each of these innocents? Both the American and the Connecticut constitutions guarantee that "no person shall be... deprived of life, liberty, or property without due process of law." Where was the due process that this September will put another estimated 50,000 Connecticut 5-year-old kids under school arrest for the next 13 years of their lives?

Saying it's for their own good only adds insult to injury. Their parents should decide what is good for their own children. If the parents choose to send them to school, that's their decision.

The DCF claims that they never seek custody unless a child is in "imminent danger." If a child is being starved or beaten to death, they should be protected from the assailant, as should any such victim. Nutritional neglect, for example, could pose an imminent danger.

But educational neglect? Imminent danger? The next doctor who shouts, "Quick! Get this kid some Chaucer! And a line of algebra problems, stat!" will be the first.

I can't think of any possible definition of educational neglect that excludes publicly and privately schooled students, or one that could pose any imminent danger to anybody, let alone the student. Can you?

Then why do we let our government take our children away from us, the very children we have freed from their jail-like schools?

It's time to get government out of the forced education business. It's time to separate school and state.

Originally published on June 13, 2007

Our state law requires children to be instructed in "reading, writing, spelling, English grammar, geography, arithmetic and United States history and in citizenship, including a study of the town, state and federal governments." (Conn. Gen. Stat. 10-184)

How hard is that, really?

Each of those subjects by themselves could require a lifetime to master. In principle, each of us could be deemed by law to have failed in the instruction. If you've ever read a word you didn't know, written something that just wasn't very good, or failed to be the national spelling bee champion, then your parents violated the law and shirked their responsibility to have you properly instructed.

Some of those subjects can simply never be mastered. The Wikipedia entry for "geography" lists more than 25 different subcategories ranging from geomorphology and oceanography to the geography of religion, geopolitics, geomatics and geodesy.

Do you know all that?

Even simple-seeming arithmetic can't be mastered. Microsoft's 2007 version of Excel, for example, reports 850 times 77.1 as 100,000, instead of 65,535. In commenting on that display error, a blog on the website for the software package Mathematica notes that arithmetic is hard to get right, and takes the case of multiplication.

Can you multiply two numbers? The way you do it for, say, two 20-digit numbers would take you 400 pairwise multiplications. But some smarter algorithms could do it in about 80 pair-wise multiplications. If you don't know those algorithms, have you failed arithmetic?

Arithmetic could also be held to include the field of number theory, which to this day has many unsolved problems that have defied solution by the brightest minds for hundreds of years. Virtually all cryptography is based on the idea that it is very hard to factor large numbers.

Are we all failures?

Should arithmetic even be required by law anymore, when calculators fit in wristwatches and cellphones and every store uses barcodes and computers instead of paper and pencil? Why must children be forced to learn long division? Should they also be forced to learn how to take the square root of large numbers by hand?

How much United States history must be required by law?

The Simpsons explains.

When Apu Nahassapeemapetilan applies for his American citizenship, the proctor asks him in the oral exam to explain the cause of the Civil War.

"Actually, there were numerous causes," Apu replies. "Aside from the obvious schism between the abolitionists and the anti-abolitionists, there were economic factors, both domestic and inter-"

"Wait, wait." The proctor cuts him off. "Just say slavery."

"Slavery it is, sir."

Of course, we are not all experts in each of these fields. Let us graciously give the law the (unrequited) benefit of the doubt and suppose that it calls only for a working knowledge of these fields. Shouldn't any fifth-grader be able to pass a simple exam on such topics? More to the point, what should happen to those who can? Should we continue to force them to attend school for an extra seven years, a full 50 percent more of their life to date at that point?

Each graduating senior has received education over his or her lifetime that cost at least $150,000.

But what was the value of the education they actually received? Given the choice, how many of them would have preferred to study and work on their own in exchange for a lump-sum cash payment of $88,000 when they are 11 years old? Some of them could have studied and gone to college early. Some of them could have earned even more money and learned real world skills through on-the-job training had they been allowed to work. Some of them could have learned on their own at home, through the internet or through books that need not be approved by any school board or committee. And some of them could have just enjoyed their childhood a while longer.

Instead, we imprison truants.

We punish employers willing to hire kids who want to work during school hours.

We impose busywork bureaucratic requirements and the constant threat of prosecution on parents who want to home-school their children.

And the only time children are allowed to enjoy their childhood anymore is on snow days and school vacations.

Originally published on November 8, 2007

SCHOOL DAZE: THROW OUT PUBLIC EDUCATION

Let's kick off the New Year with some out-of-the-box think-ing. What if we didn't have public education here in Fairfield County? What if we separated school and state and let educa-tion be entirely a private matter?

If you hadn't resolved to be more open-minded this year, you might have dismissed this as foolishness. *After all, every-body knows without government we would all be illiterate bums. Privatizing education? Come on. It can't be done, people wouldn't do it even if they could, and it shouldn't be done even if people would.*

It can't be done? Consider Sundays. As far as I know, every single public school at all grade levels is closed on Sundays. Nei-ther the State of Connecticut, nor any of the 23 municipalities in Fairfield County regularly contributes educational information to anybody on each of the 52 Sundays throughout each year. Yet kids still learn. They go to Sunday school at church. They go to Hebrew school in a synagogue. They go to Chinese school or Russian school. What's more, it's not a cookie-cutter curriculum; they learn what their parents want them to learn.

Marshall Fritz, director of the Separation of School and State Alliance, puts it succinctly: "Two centuries ago, Americans ended government undermining of parents by removing gov-ernment involvement in Sunday school. Now we need to do the same with Monday school, Tuesday school, Wednesday school, etc."

And remember, there is no summer semester for most pub-lic school students. Yet kids don't seem to get lost. Parents send them to camps and retreats and are somehow magically able to fill the time they would have spent trapped behind brick.

Fine, sure, the cynic says. *It can in principle be done, but people wouldn't do it. It's too much hassle and it's too expensive.* Really? Consider martial arts. There is a dojo of some sort on almost every street. You can choose from tae kwon do, judo, karate, and more. Consider piano lessons. Or guitar. Or saxophone. Pick any musical instrument, stroll into your local grocery store, and pick your teacher from the bulletin board. Instructors provide these services precisely because parents want them. Imagine the same with history or English or math.

It's less hassle because there is more accountability. You can't fire your kid's English teacher even if they tell your son or daughter that candy canes are shaped like the letter J for Jesus—as some teachers have been caught doing—and your family is Jewish or Hindu, or just don't want your kid, and other kids, being taught Christianity with your tax dollars. (Besides, the letter-J claim is false; candy canes were bent to represent a shepherd's staff.) Imagine you could switch private instructors for any reason or for no reason at all. And it's less expensive because there is more competition for your dollar.

Still, the cynic scoffs, *even though it can be done, and even though people would do it, or at least would have the choice, it still shouldn't be done, because then poor people wouldn't be able to afford an education, or parents would make their kids work instead of learn, and that's just not fair.*

Talk about fairness. Is it fair to force kids to attend school even if a gifted student could learn the material and pass the final exam after the first class? Is it fair to tax childless adults to pay for a service they do not need?

And consider the poor. Is it fair to force them to do what you want them to do, rather than what they would prefer? Suppose they could move to a nicer apartment with the money that's being paid for their kids' school. Suppose one of the parents could quit a minimum wage job and homeschool the kids. Is it fair that you won't even give them that choice?

A year of education for a child in a Fairfield County public school costs about $13,000. A year of full-time minimum wage is $16,000 in income—before taxes. If the parents simply received the $13,000 as cash, they could work part-time, homeschool their kids, teach them the values they believe, and still come out thousands of dollars ahead.

Consider the children, the concerned cynic sings. *If parents fail to have them taught the basic knowledge that public schools provide then they will be unemployable as adults.*

In other words, we are putting children through a mandatory 12-year program to make them better workers. Is that really what education is supposed to be about? Is that what the children would choose to spend the money on? At $13,000 per year times 12 years, each high school graduate has received education that cost about $150,000. How many of them would have preferred, as adults, in retrospect, to have maybe received only $10,000, enough to pay a tutor to teach them basic reading and arithmetic, and spend the rest of the money on cars, houses, seed capital for a business, or just tons of candy canes? Is it fair that they should have no choice in the matter?

Public education has mandatory attendance, is funded by mandatory taxes, and is provided by a mandatory monopoly by the government. Perhaps some of these restrictions could be relaxed.

This new year, let's resolve to think for ourselves.

Originally published on January 3, 2008

Is Harry Potter a Libertarian?

On page 357 of *Harry Potter and the Deathly Hallows*, author J.K. Rowling reveals **(spoiler alert!!!)** that the newly deceased headmaster of the wizard school Hogwarts, Albus Dumbledore, was a brimming socialist-communist in his teenage years.

It's not an accident or a needless plot twist. It's a powerful climax that's been building for years. The damning letter by the young Dumbledore first appears on the only page of the final book numbered with three consecutive odd prime numbers. And the words themselves could just as easily have been written by Karl Marx, Vladimir Lenin or any far-left liberal today: "Yes, we have been given power and yes, that power gives us the right to rule, but it also gives us responsibilities over the ruled. We must stress this point, it will be the foundation stone upon which we build. Where we are opposed, as we surely will be, this must be the basis of all our counter-arguments. We seize control FOR THE GREATER GOOD." (Capital letters in original.)

The young Dumbledore had no qualms about harming the few to benefit the many. He had no misgivings about initiating the use of force for whatever he considers the greater good. Today, socialized medicine, Social Security, Medicare, Medicaid and hundreds of other social programs are based on this exact same thinking. And we seem to vote for that thinking every time.

But Harry Potter doesn't. Potter is not like Dumbledore. For seven books and thousands of pages, Potter never used violence except in self-defense, and he always tried to save the lives; even those of his enemies. His tale is one of a constant and heartrending struggle to prevent sacrifice even by his dearest friends, rather than a cold-blooded calculation of whom and how best to sacrifice for the greater good. Potter spends much of the seventh book convincing as many as people as possible not to get involved in the central conflicts at all.

Is Potter a libertarian? One of the shortest definitions of libertarianism is an opposition to the initiation of force. If you want to become a member of the Libertarian Party of Connecticut, you must sign this pledge: "I hereby certify that I do not believe in or advocate the initiation of force to achieve political, social, or economic goals." Self-defense, of course, is not an initiation of force. But think eminent domain abuse, asset forfeiture laws and prohibition. Think taxes. Think Iraq.

This question applies to us more than any other part of America. Just as Fairfield County is often the nation's yardstick on Iraq and taxes, it also was one of the final battlegrounds of witchcraft in the 17th century. According to the Connecticut Humanities Council, "If one excludes the events in Salem from consideration, Connecticut was the witchcraft center of New England."

Indeed, according to a report put out last December by the Office of Legislative Research by the Connecticut General Assembly, our Puritanical state had been indicting, trying, and executing early Harry Potters by means of Blue Laws, written more than 30 years before the infamous Salem witch trials of 1692 executed 21 people in the space of two seasons. Unlike the one-year Massachusetts frenzy, Connecticut fed a long and steady diet of witches, approximately one trial per year until 1662 when our law was changed to require at least two simultaneous witnesses to the alleged bewitching. Then for thirty years, only a handful made it to court.

But in 1692, likely as a reaction to the Salem brouhaha, Connecticut awakened from its relatively slow trickle to accuse eight citizens of witchcraft. Of those eight, five were from Fairfield and one from Stamford.

Once again and as usual, Fairfield County was in a unique place, at a unique time, to determine the destiny of the free world. We were essentially the last testing ground of witch hunts. And we acted as honorably as we could, given the law we were supposed to enforce. As far as I can tell, all six Fairfield County defendants were acquitted or freed.

350 years later, the arrival of the seventh book by J.K. Rowling brings witchcraft and libertarianism back to Fairfield County. To me, a lifelong libertarian who ran for Congress on the Libertarian ticket last year, the phrase "greater good" screams out socialism. And I am not surprised that it is a young Dumbledore that is presented in this light. Most far-left liberals, like many of the readers of this paper, are young, well-educated, and fiery, just like the young Dumbledore, just like the young Lenin. Once the initiation of force is morally permissible, young, educated, powerful people tend to think they are the best to determine how to use that power...for the greater good.

But the initiation of force is not morally permissible. And Harry Potter understood that from birth. Eventually, so does Dumbledore. It happens on page 716.

Is it a coincidence that July 16, 1979 was the day Saddam Hussein came to power in Iraq? Or that a year later to the day, Ronald Reagan won the Republican nomination for president and went on to strike, arguably, the greatest blows against communism and socialism of all time?

On page 716, Dumbledore explains the feelings that I suspect most liberals have. "Oh, I have a few scruples," he laments in what is either a return from death or a vision in Potter's mind. "I assuaged my conscience with empty words. It would all be for the greater good, and any harm done would be repaid a hundredfold in benefits for wizards."

I thought I was the first to notice this libertarian bent on the part of probably the most widely read non-Biblical hero of all time. But it turns out others have written on this subject before. University of Tennessee law professor Benjamin Barton wrote an article last year for the *Michigan Law Review* called "Harry Potter and the Half-Crazed Bureaucracy" in which he analyzed the hidden libertarian messages from the first six books.

This message has roots, and roots that trace back earlier than the 1997 publication of the first Potter book, earlier than the war of good and evil fought in the 1980s, earlier even than the 17th century witchcraft woes and the 15th century discovery of the new, free world. Libertarianism is the oldest, strongest message on earth. You feel it in your bones, your stomach, and your heart.

Perhaps Potter's final message is that it is time to let the message of self-reliance and freedom bubble to your mind, your arms and your mouth.

Originally published on August 1, 2007

Do you know that feeling of instant camaraderie you get when another person shares a deep passion of yours? You may not even know their real name or age or where they live but to you, the shared characteristic speaks volumes about their soul. I feel an immediate kinship with someone if I find out they are a libertarian, or if they're a Celtics fan, or if they have ever owned a Commodore Amiga.

The first two are obvious signs of good taste, strong values, and a sense of history. But who on Earth is Amiga, how did she ever rise to the rank of Commodore, and how can someone own her?

The Amiga was my secret weapon. It was a personal computer decades ahead of its time. In the early 1980s, I used the Amiga to edit videos and make cartoons as extra credit for classes in school. It had thousands of colors when its main competition had, at best, sixteen. It multi-tasked and it did so without crashing, something both Macs and PCs still struggle with. It had multiple virtual screens, each with different resolution, as if there were several computers sharing the same monitor.

And the games! The graphics, the sound, the intensity. One of the first games my dad and I played on it was a detective game where you type in what to do using regular English sentences and then watch as the characters on screen act it out, if you get it right. We got about five screens in with commands like "open the door" and "walk left" and then were stymied for months at a place where the right answer turned out to be "hide behind the couch."

I programmed on the Amiga. My first computer had been a Timex Sinclair with one kilobyte of memory that often broke or got accidentally unplugged. I had to reprogram my virtual Monopoly game from scratch every time—the code quickly became optimized as I learned about subroutines and procedures to minimize the amount of retyping. On the Amiga, most of my time was spent moving "sprites" and "bobs," Amiga-speak for two types of graphics, either fast or slow, that would float across the screen.

The Amiga had the world's first word processor with the now-ubiquitous ruler and button strips up top. Before that program, it was hard to imagine how a computer could improve on a typewriter. Most word processing programs at the time simply showed text and you had to use weird button combinations to do things. The Amiga essentially introduced WYSIWYG: What You See Is What You Get.

Much like the Libertarian Party and the Boston Celtics, the Commodore Amiga has been a source of great disappointment to me for the past 20 years. The Libertarian Party, as opposed to the libertarian philosophy, never elected a single federal official. The Celtics never hoisted another championship banner. And the Commodore Amiga didn't take over the world.

In all three cases, the killer was a combination of a lack of leadership and of being too far ahead of their time. The Libertarian Party didn't really focus on electing candidates as much as it did on growing membership, awareness, and education. The Celtics suffered through poor owners, and managers with itchy trigger fingers who traded away players such as Joe Johnson and Chauncey Billups while they were still young. And the Amiga was a great computer that was unfortunately owned by Commodore, which didn't see the jewel in their midst and, despite modest success in Europe, let this amazing technology wilt away.

There is cause for hope. The Libertarian Party, realizing that by now most people have at least a passing acquaintance with libertarianism (one character on Desperate Housewives even described himself as a libertarian, saying he believes in minimizing the power of the state and maximizing individual freedom), last year changed its focus to actually electing winnable candidates. Yours truly ran as a Libertarian candidate in our district last year to all sorts of successful measures, except at the polls.

The Boston Celtics completely reversed course this summer, moving from a youth-centered squad to a veteran team with three All-Stars. They acquired one of the best basketball players of all time in Kevin Garnett and one of the best pure shooters of all time in Ray Allen, the former Husky standout. They went from having the second-worst record in the league last year to being a championship contender.

And to complete the trifecta, Commodore has risen from the ashes and will be moving in to 263 Tresser Boulevard in Stamford. They no longer own the Amiga brand or its technology but they are run by coders and gamers who grew up on the Amiga and remember its unique niche in computer lore. And they're not just selling kitschy computers from the 80s, though that "vintage" product is on their website. They're selling souped-up Windows PCs optimized for gaming.

What can I say. I feel a kinship toward them. Deep in my heart, I also suspect they are libertarians and Celtic fans.

Originally published on September 13, 2007

JENA, JUNTA, JESSE, AND GEORGE

If we understand the common thread between scores of monks arrested and beaten in Burma and the rationale behind civil rights activists like Jesse Jackson in defending six violent black teenagers in Louisiana, we will get a glimpse into the mind of George W. Bush and the war in Iraq.

The so-called Jena 6 are six black youths charged with the attempted murder of a white teenager last December. Jackson and an estimated fifty thousand others marched on the Louisiana town of less than 3,000 to protest the "unfair" treatment of these alleged criminals. That would be like one million marching on Greenwich (population 62,000). Why did all these people march? Was it really in support of half a dozen violent people?

One of them, Mychal Bell, had already been tried and convicted as an adult but had his verdict overturned because he should have been, and now will be, tried as a juvenile. Did thousands of people really descend on this sleepy landlocked village of five square miles to support the incarcerated Bell?

It's a complex question why and how marches, rallies and protests happen. Look at what's happening in Burma. The Asian country became independent in 1948 but was basically ruled by a single person until 1988, and his military junta after that. In 1990, the junta refused to hand over power to the newly democratically elected government, and it's been under military rule ever since.

This summer, Buddhist monks began what seemed to be a mild protest against high commodity prices, specifically fuel. This is not your typical American protest over high gas prices and "profiteering" private companies. In Burma, the government sets gas prices by fiat. It started with only a few hundred protesters and resulted with dozens of arrests but no stalling. Eventually it grew as more and more people began to march, culminating in estimates of probably a hundred thousand pro-democracy demonstrators marching, of which only a small minority are monks.

Twenty years ago, Burma had even larger demonstrations which resulted in the junta simply shooting and killing thousands. It may be approaching a similar situation now.

Why did thousands join what had been a small protest against high gas prices in a country with a history of violence against peaceful demonstrations? Why did thousands in Jena protest what had been a local arrest?

These protests are similar to the state income tax protests of 1991 in which you or someone you know probably marched on Hartford. More than 40,000 people crowded the Capitol's south lawn to yell, "Repeal! Repeal!" before the tax became law. Connecticut has a proud libertarian history of opposing taxes and big government. The legislature reversed the law, but Gov. Lowell Weicker vetoed the reversal, and legislators fell one vote shy of overturning the veto. But at least we marched.

Marches and protests seem to balloon out from a single small event. Even the Boston Tea Party stemmed from a three-pence tax exemption on tea to the East India Company. In Hartford, it began with the income tax but ballooned into a protest of big, bad government. People held up signs of Hitler. Speeches talked not about Democrats and Republicans but "good guys and bad guys." In Burma, it ballooned from gas prices to political freedom.

In Jena, it has become about race in general and whether blacks are treated equally under the law. That's a critical issue, but in this case, it seems more tacked-on than a natural ballooning from the original incident.

Three months before the six attacked their victim, a group of white high school students hung nooses from a tree. No charges were filed against them, though they faced some academic disciplinary action. That may seem unfair but the noose-hangers did not violate a single federal or state statute on hate or any other crime because the teens could not, according to federal standards, be certified as adults. It was not a crime and therefore the fact the noose-hangers were not charged was not a decision based on race, as the Jena 6 supporters allege.

Also, the kid the six attacked was not one of those who hung the nooses and, according to a U.S. attorney, of the 40 statements taken during the attack, not one mentioned the nooses.

Between the noose incident and the beating, there were a series of race-motivated attacks and retaliatory attacks and Jackson and company allege that the white attackers did not get the same harsh treatment as the six. But just because I get beat up and the guy gets away certainly doesn't mean I can beat up someone else of his race and get away with it!

The ironic thing is that Jackson's rationale mirrors Bush's rationale in invading Iraq. We attacked Iraq using 9/11 as a pretext even though Iraq wasn't involved in 9/11 in any way. Like the Jena 6, we attacked people who weren't responsible for an attack on us, and we probably would have wanted to attack them anyway, but we use the earlier tragedy to justify a new one. And Iraq has ballooned into a seemingly never-ending occupation. Who would have thought that Jackson and Bush would use the same logic?

Originally published on October 4, 2007

WERE THE ORIGINAL HEBREWS FREEDOM FIGHTERS?

Earlier this month, conservative author Ann Coulter said Jews need to be "perfected" into Christians. Iranian president Mahmoud Ahmadinejad routinely denies the Holocaust and says Israel needs to be "wiped off the map." Of *Vanity Fair's* recent "hundred most powerful people," more than half were Jewish when counted by the *Jerusalem Post* and checked by *New York Magazine*.

I have heard that anti-Semitism is the only word that expresses racism against a single specific ethnicity, and while I don't know if that's true, I can't think of another example. I try to imagine what it would be like to hate a particular kind of person. The best I can come up with is communists.

I hate communism by any name: totalitarianism, dictatorship, socialism, oligarchy, fascism. Yet when I meet communists, I believe they are merely misguided. If I speak with them, and they are reasonable, but do not change their minds, I feel sad, as if I have failed, as if it is my fault for not finding the right words to show them the truth they were longing to see.

But I could hardly imagine myself ever being so insulting as saying communists need to be perfected into libertarians, or so duplicitous as claiming no communists died under Stalin's rule, or so murderous as declaring that communists need to be wiped off the map. I couldn't imagine a more boring activity than counting presumed communists on the lists of powerful people.

I pity communists in that they do not know the joys of liberty. It's like trying to explain color to someone who only sees shades of gray.

I wonder how they feel about me? I've gotten some hate mail, and I've heard of other libertarians who have too. I've assumed defenders of totalitarian government get their fair share as well, but perhaps the emotions some communists and their ilk feel for libertarians isn't the mirror image of pity. Perhaps they truly feel something closer to hate.

Perhaps they have to. I believe communists live an inner contradiction every day. Outwardly, they profess the need to share, spread wealth, and so on. But deep in their hearts, how could they not understand that sharing and spreading must be voluntary to be meaningful? I believe communists sense this problem, at least subconsciously, and when promoters of liberty point it out, they must banish the thought if they are to maintain their illusion. It takes an inwardly strong communist to reasonably discuss freedom, and if they have that strength, they are more than halfway to being libertarians already. Emails from such readers are a joy. I often have lengthy exchanges with them, and I love every minute of it.

For those without the moral strength to at least consider the contradictions, they are threatened by cognitive dissonance, and perhaps to resolve their inner struggle, they must hate not only the message but the messenger.

Perhaps that's why many people hate Jews so much.

In his recent book *How to Read the Bible*, James L. Kugel draws from ancient interpreters and modern biblical scholars. One question that comes up halfway through is, where did the Hebrews come from? He describes the El Amarna letters discovered 120 years ago, tablets written by Canaanites around the time when the Jews were supposedly invading Canaan. There is no mention of an invading army.

But the local rulers often complain of the apiru or the habiru, referring to a group of rebellious peasants. It is no stretch to see the similarity to the word Hebrew. One theory is that Hebrews started as a grass-roots movement of Canaanite revolutionaries, perhaps stoked by tales of escape by their brothers from Egypt, perhaps with their disparate groups joined together by a common belief in a new, previously unknown God. But ethnically, they were the same as the people they overthrew. As Kugel puts it, "We have met the Canaanites and they are us."

Perhaps, then, the Hebrews launched the first popular libertarian revolt. (Was the American Revolution the last?)

About two thousand years ago, a Gentile who wished to become a Jew asked Rabbi Hillel, one of the most famous Jewish sages and the namesake for countless synagogues, to explain the entire Torah while standing on one foot—in other words, in a very few words. Hillel replied, "What is hateful to you, do not do to your fellow. This is the whole Law; the rest is commentary."

There can probably be no better summary of libertarianism.

If this theory is true—that the Jews essentially arose as freedom fighters—there are a great many ironies today. Modern Jews tend to be socialists, particularly in Israel, where the tradition of kibbutzim, or collectivist living, has long been an ideological staple, counting at its peak 1 in 15 Israelis as followers. Yet the Israelis are still hated, I believe, for the values of freedom and revolt that their very existence still represent.

Is it not the same with the United States? We founded the world's first libertarian country but have become just another large government with an oppressed populace. Isn't it equally ironic that some people can continue to hate the freedom represented by Americans even as those very freedoms are being taken away from us?

I know I will receive hate mail for this piece. I will get furious emails from communists calling themselves liberals, totalitarians calling themselves conservatives, apologists calling themselves patriots, anti-Semites calling themselves religious, and kibbutz-niks calling themselves offended Jews.

I do hope I also receive emails from similar people with reasoned moral objections to libertarianism, and maybe another productive dialogue can start. No one will get perfected, because liberty isn't about utopia. It's about doing the right thing.

Originally published on October 25, 2007

One hundred and ninety-two years ago this month, Connecticut almost seceded from the United States of America because of an unconstitutional, overseas war that was infringing on our liberties. Sound familiar?

Feb. 13, 1815 was the day Connecticut didn't secede. The unimaginatively named War of 1812 had officially been over since Christmas but because the peace treaty had been signed in Ghent, Belgium, and because internet service in those times was spotty at best, it had taken almost two months for the news to reach our shores.

During that time, soon-to-be-president Andrew Jackson defeated the British in New Orleans in a stunning military victory that was entirely unnecessary. Neither side knew that the war was already over. The British retreated to Biloxi, Miss., where they captured Fort Bowyer on Feb. 12, a strategically important fort that Jackson had garrisoned with hundreds of officers, declaring that "ten thousand men cannot take it." The British had less than 1,000 men. They took it.

Politicians still underestimate the power of the enemy, a fact we're reminded of as we approach the four-year anniversary of the date when Bush declared the end of major combat operations in Iraq.

Back to February 1815. New England had sent a delegation to Washington to "negotiate terms"—it was considering seceding from the Union. Connecticut had been independent for hundreds of years and still considered itself free, and it didn't like what its federal government was doing. Connecticut had been a state for 37 years at that point.

Age is relative, and Connecticut has had several makeovers in the intervening decades. If we judge by when we adopted our current constitution (a little like judging age by the date of one's last facelift, admittedly), then we are only 42 years old; we ratified our state constitution in 1965.

But let's return to the weekend of Feb. 11 and 12, 1815. On the 13th, the news that the War of 1812 was over would be everywhere, but the weekend before, people felt as people feel now: we've been fighting too long for no reason and we've had too many of our liberties taken from us by the politicians we entrusted to protect them.

One of those lost liberties was our ability to export and trade overseas. "If you won't sell to us," the thinking goes, "we won't sell to you. Ha!"

Trade restrictions have never worked. They always make the restricting country worse off. It hit Connecticut especially hard.

We still have trade restrictions, ranging from tariffs to import and export quotas to the various embargoes and sanctions we've had on Iraq, Iran, South Africa, etc., none of which worked, and all of which hurt Americans.

Even more poignant to Connecticut at the time was conscription. The war had dragged on for so long that citizens were being drafted to fight.

Connecticut wouldn't stand for it. In 1814, it secretly convened delegations from the five New England states to determine what should be done. It came to be known as the Hartford Convention. It was so secret, we have still never found a single thorough record of the proceedings, other than the report and resolutions adopted on Jan. 5, 1815. Much of the debate centered on whether New England should secede. Had the federal government overstepped its constitutional authority so much that it should be thrown out?

This is exactly the question facing modern Americans, as the federal government has gotten monstrously large, mainly in the last few decades.

Yet, where is our Hartford Convention today? Where is the uproar over Iraq and over all of our freedoms that have been taken from us? Patriot Act I and II. The Military Commissions Act. Mountains of Executive Orders. "National security letters" that can force us to do things without a judge's oversight. Warrantless wiretapping. The constant indignities we go through just to take a 30-minute airplane flight. Why aren't we secretly convening delegates? Or are we?

The final report of the Hartford Convention proposed amendments to the U.S. Constitution to prohibit any trade embargo lasting more than 60 days, and to require a two-thirds congressional majority to declare war or interrupt foreign trade in any way.

The conflict in Iraq was never even declared a war by Congress. Even without the Hartford Convention's amendments, it is an unconstitutional conflict.

Why don't we do anything? We have gotten hooked on federal handouts. You can at least in principle stop an addiction at any time by refusing to pay for the stuff you get. But the federal government has a sneakier setup. It doesn't provide services for money. That would make ending those services too easy. Instead, it takes money directly from the people, and then doles it back out to them in the form of services, provided the people meet certain requirements.

You want federal funding for education? You have to comply with burdensome regulations and deal with the federal Department of Education.

You want federal funding to build supportive housing for the homeless? You have to go out and count the number of homeless people. Just last week we sent hundreds of volunteers into the streets of Fairfield County, not looking to help the homeless, but to count them.

It's like a pusher who takes everybody's money, whether they want the drugs or not, and then gives free drugs to people who do personal favors for him. Our representatives spend far too much time bragging about how much money they "bring back" to the state, instead of doing their job to make sure the federal government doesn't take it in the first place.

So what do we do now?

Once the New Englanders of 1815 had their resolutions in hand, they sent a team of negotiators to Washington to demand changes and threaten secession.

Those negotiators got to Washington in early February. On Feb. 13, newspapers announced that the war was over. The negotiators had no choice but to go home. They had no more leverage.

How can we stop the war now?

One lesson we learned from 1815 is that if you allow the federal government to grow, then, like any weed, it will.

But, just like it did nearly two centuries ago, New England is starting to stand up to the federal government. Maine recently rejected the federal Real ID Act, which would essentially create a national ID card, becoming the first state in the union to buck the feds. New Hampshire is now a destination for thousands of libertarians who are part of the Free State Project, which wants to bring freedom back to America one state at a time. Even Massachusetts nearly repealed its state income tax a few years ago to reduce the overall size of government.

Where is Connecticut in all this? Why aren't we leading the charge once again for more freedom and less federal intrusion onto our liberties? We have one of the strongest libertarian histories of any state.

It's time for another Hartford Convention.

Originally published on February 15, 2007

Last week the far-left Middlebury Institute, which wants Vermont to secede from the United States, joined with the far-right League of the South, which essentially wants to re-establish the Confederacy, for a two-day secessionist convention. Why wasn't Connecticut represented? For that matter, why wasn't Fairfield County?

Secession simply means withdrawing from a distant political power and governing yourself. When it happens halfway around the world, it is called self-determination, self-government, or democracy, and we've sent lots of our own soldiers and fire-power over to help. When it happens here, it is called a revolution or a civil war.

But it shouldn't be. Donald Livingston, an Emory University professor of philosophy (who has some ties to the League of the South) put it nicely a few years ago: "There was no American Revolution, but a war of secession. And there was no American Civil War, but a war to suppress secession."

He also notes that it used to be libertarian Yankees that were the ones most likely to call for secession. For a period of time in the 19th century, New England threatened to secede about once every five years. Then the Civil War put a real damper on anybody who tried to secede from Lincoln's America.

But that same American drive for self-determination that won us our freedom two hundred years ago never died. It was merely napping. And in recent years, it's started to awaken. In the past ten years, we've seen people try to create, through secession, the Republic of Texas, the Republic of Cascadia in the

Pacific Northwest, a sovereign Hawaii, and, last year, a separate Alaska, in addition to the two biggest movements of Vermont and the South.

What is it about the past decade or so that has spawned so many distinct movements to secede from the U.S.? What is happening to make even socialists and paleoconservatives get along? It's looking an awful lot like rats fleeing a sinking ship.

Phillip Seff notes in his book *Our Fascinating Earth* that this skill of rats was observed two thousand years ago by Pliny the Elder, who wrote that "when a building is about to fall down, all the rats desert it." Seff explains why rats seem to be able to anticipate aquatic disaster. "Rats live in the deepest recesses of the ship, in the bilge," he notes, an area that is essentially inaccessible to the crew, and so they are the first to have their nests flooded. They issue shrill cries of alarm and "build up into a large, frightened mass of rodents making a panicky exodus." The upstairs crew sees the rats deserting the ship even though as far as they can tell the ship itself still looks fine.

The analogy is pretty striking. The secessionist movements today are not, as a rule, being led by powerful politicians, captains of industry or famous celebrities. They are led and strengthened by everyday people who see their wallets pinched, their phones tapped, and their speech silenced by a powerful central government, one that was never intended to get so big. And, being Americans, they want their freedom back.

It would be hard for Connecticut as a whole to secede. Last year, an attempt to put an initiative on the Alaskan ballot to secede was ruled unconstitutional by the Supreme Court of Alaska. And of course, we still remember the bloodshed that resulted the last time a state actually tried to leave the Union.

But perhaps it is possible for towns and cities in Fairfield County to form a political entity and disassociate from the rest of Connecticut. After all, for this, precedent is on our side: West Virginia seceded from Virginia during the Civil War.

Our county has about one-quarter of the total population of the state and includes five of the nine most populous cities, including Bridgeport, the largest. Yet we pay, by a variety of measures, for about half of Connecticut's budget. For some of our wealthier towns the disparity is even greater: Greenwich, Stamford, Fairfield, New Canaan, and Westport combine to pay for 25 percent of the whole state budget despite having about 8 percent of the population.

Fairfield County is only about 10 percent of the total land area of Connecticut but even as a separate state it wouldn't be too small: It would be about half the size of Rhode Island or about ten times the size of Washington, D.C.

Just imagine what we could do without the burdens of the entire state of Connecticut, and much of the rest of the United States, on our shoulders. We could reject the federal "grants" that come with so many strings and handcuffs attached. We could constitutionally prevent an income tax from ever being levied. We could educate our children, build our roads, and care for our elderly in any way we choose, not how distant politicians think we should. Cities like Stamford and Bridgeport would prosper and we would be known as the Fairfield Miracle—all for merely getting out before it was too late.

And what of the many state politicians we leave behind to try to finally fix their budget woes now that their golden egg has hatched? They, like the fabled captain, would have to go down with the ship.

Originally published on October 11, 2007

Greenwich recently celebrated its birthday. The town is either 367, 342, 335, 321 or one billion years old, depending on when you start counting.

The official date commemorated last week was July 18, 1640 when two settlers, representing the New Haven colony, bought Old Greenwich from Native Americans for "twenty-five coates." Much like the famous purchase of Manhattan for $24 worth of trinkets 14 years earlier, it's not clear if sellers were actually the people who owned the land or were merely the ones who happened to occupy it at the time.

Anybody can found a town. It's like discovering a model. There she is! But the next step is making sure no one else can claim her.

It wasn't until May 11, 1665 that the Hartford General Assembly declared Greenwich a separate township. For years, they had tried to make it part of Stamford. The modern-day state income tax and often proposed wealth and millionaire's taxes are a continued attempt to essentially do the same thing: make the wealthy property owners pay more than their fair share.

The area of Greenwich called Horseneck, and including its famous Tod's Point beach, didn't become part of the town until it was purchased from the increasingly real estate-savvy Native Americans in 1672. But that was just the contract date. The closing on the land took place in 1686.

So just how old is Greenwich? There are already four possible dates from which to judge: the founding, the declaration as a township, the purchase date of the remaining tract and the date the title actually transferred.

Or the date the land was formed. If I read the inscription right at the geological exhibit in Greenwich's Bruce Museum, there's a type of rock called the Fordham gneiss that is over a billion years old—dating from the time, if I understand correctly, when Connecticut was still connected to Africa. The Fordham gneiss occurs nowhere else in the state of Connecticut except for one little corner of northwestern Greenwich.

The word "gneiss" is an old mining term meaning decayed, rotten or worthless material. You might think it is insulting for Connecticut's poshest town to be built on such a rock. You'd be wrong. It is actually quite flattering.

The genius of humanity comes from taking the apparently worthless material around it and making it into something useful. The genius comes from trade and an unwavering dedication to providing value to others on a voluntary basis. Allowing that genius to shine as brightly as possible is nearly the definition of libertarianism.

Is Greenwich the state's most libertarian town? It headquarters a litany of hedge funds, one of the two greatest creative industries in existence today, the other being the internet. Why those two? They have among the least regulation. It's hard to be creative in health care when you have to get the approval of so many layers of government.

What is the political structure that tends to result in such libertarianism? What features does it share with the United States in general, still basically the freest country in the world despite the fact that it is much less free today than it was before?

I think one feature is the number of people in government. With power concentrated into the hands of a few, oligarchy and effective dictatorship are not far behind.

Greenwich's Representative Town Meeting has 230 elected officials, making it the fifth largest legislative body in the United States. Only Congress itself and three state legislatures have more.

So many eyes mean two things, both beneficial: more gridlock and less sneaky maneuvering. It becomes harder for government to do anything that doesn't have widespread appeal among a variety of supermajorities. And it becomes harder to slip things past the voters when there are so many people watching what happens. Almost anything that makes things harder for government to control your life is a good thing.

So happy birthday, Greenwich, however old you are.

Originally published on July 26, 2007

GOVERNMENT IS THE DEVIL'S BUSINESS

For 400 years, the "devil's advocate" was a lawyer appointed by the Roman Catholic Church to argue against promoting a candidate to sainthood, like a pro bono attorney for the prosecution instead of the defense. The devil's advocate argued, even if he didn't believe it, that the alleged miracles didn't actually happen or happened in a non-miraculous way, or that the evidence was phony or weak or suspect. In other words, the devil's advocate personified due diligence.

How well did it work? Even though the devil's advocate was only pretending to object, the mere fact that there was someone there to object at all kept the number of saints appointed to a total of 143 in the 396 years from the time the position was created in 1588 until the time the position was abolished in 1983—a rate of about one saint every three years.

What was the effect of removing this small hurdle of a single skeptic?

The floodgates opened. Nearly 500 people became saints in the two and a half decades since then, about 20 saints per year.

Have we really been fortunate enough to live in the most miraculous time of all, an era that, by this measure, is 60 times as miraculous as usual?

Or perhaps this illustrates the power of even a single doubting Thomas.

The original doubting Thomas and the source of the term was Thomas the Apostle. He doubted the resurrection of Jesus and demanded to feel his wounds firsthand. When he felt them and became convinced, he became known as Thomas the Believer. Thus, the original doubting Thomas ironically became the best eyewitness to the defining miracle of Christianity, which hinges on Jesus not having a corpse.

Two weeks ago, Titanic director James Cameron announced he found the tomb of Jesus. Perhaps Thomas didn't doubt enough. But at least he doubted.

How many legislators either in Connecticut or Washington, D.C. are willing to play the role of devil's advocate? How many are willing to argue that a particular bill is unconstitutional, or that the proposed cure would be worse than the disease, or even that the topic is something that should be decided voluntarily by people and not by law?

By rights, each legislator should act as the devil's advocate. When they are inaugurated, they swear to uphold the constitution. Unfortunately in most cases that seems to be the last time they mention the document.

Governor M. Jodi Rell has created a new $75,000 post in government: the Business Advocate. Oh, if only this were akin to the devil's advocate. If only this were a position to be filled by a person who would argue against every single bill, finding flaws, loopholes, errors, and downright unconstitutionality on which to defeat it. If the effect of such a post were to limit laws as effectively as the original devil's advocate limited sainthood, it would be money very well spent.

But no. Our new Business Advocate is not a position for someone who even pretends to dislike government. It is a position for someone who loves government.

And it has been filled by someone who adores government.

Rell announced last week her appointment to the post of Rob Simmons, the former second district Congressman who lost his re-election bid last November to Joe Courtney, by less than a hundred votes. According to Rell's press release, the Republican Simmons has "spent his entire career in public service."

Yet he is now responsible for "advocating" the interests of business. As Business Advocate, he is responsible for "providing information on public and private programs to assist businesses, and for targeting specific small and micro businesses for growth and providing them with programs, services, technical assistance, job training and financial assistance."

Let's play devil's advocate for a moment, since apparently no one else will.

Number 1: there should not be any public programs to assist business. Any such programs simply take money from taxpayers by force and give it to politically favored companies. By definition, businesses are supposed to operate in the free market, providing goods and services to people who are willing to pay for them. They are not supposed to be branches of government, supported by forced extraction of money from the populace.

Number 2: it should not be the government's role to provide information about private programs to assist businesses. If I run a program that assists businesses, why should you be forced to pay for my marketing budget through your taxes?

Number 3: the government should not be targeting any businesses of any size, small, micro, macro, or large. Not for any purpose, certainly not in order to provide them with "programs, services, etc." Businesses are supposed to fend for themselves, not suckle on a government breast filled with the milk of taxpayers.

Perhaps that's too pleasant an image for a devil's advocate.

Or perhaps what we libertarians advocate isn't the devil's work at all, but the most heavenly trait of all: freedom.

Originally published on March 8, 2007

World War II ended in Europe with Victory in Europe Day on May 8, 1945, 62 years ago this past Tuesday. Within two months of V.E. Day, the Stamford War Council had disbanded.

The council had been created four years earlier to control the frequent blackouts and dim-outs (street lights were turned off) prepare for possible air raids, and direct traffic and people to shelters in cases of air-raid drills. No actual air raids ever occurred, of course, though Stamford was considered a target because many of its industries converted to war work.

Looking back more than half a century, it is easy to wallow in three myths about WWII.

One myth is that before Pearl Harbor, America did nothing and feared nothing, thinking it was a European war. That's not true. The Stamford War Council was formed six months *before* the attack on Pearl Harbor. By then, much of our economy had shifted to providing materiel to those who would later be known as our Allies. We were already involved in the war—much like 9/11 wasn't the first terrorist attack on American soil, nor even the first terrorist attacks on the Twin Towers.

The danger of this first myth, of non-involvement, is that it can bring about complacency, which can lead to lapses in border security and national defense that can be exploited by our enemies.

The second myth is that America entered the war and essentially won it on behalf of the Allies. In truth, the Soviet Union did virtually all the work. America came in toward the end, and while we certainly helped bring about the war's end more quickly than might otherwise have been the case, it is possible that the Soviet Union would have won by itself even if we hadn't stepped in. But there's no way we would have won without the Soviets.

One of the war's great battles was D-Day, when the U.S. and the Allies invaded Normandy and defeated 67,000 Germans who were, according to the *Encyclopedia Britannica* mostly "poorly equipped, second-rate troops." The bulk of the Germans' top troops were in what seemed (to them) a more likely area for the Allies to invade.

By contrast, the Soviets defended themselves deep inside their own country in Stalingrad, against 390,000 of the best the German army had to throw at them, and won. For every American life lost in the war, the Soviets lost 80. These numbers come from J.K. Dykman of the Eisenhower Institute, who also points out that our northwest Europe and Italy fronts saw 140,000 American soldiers killed out of about 2,000,000; they fought against 1,500,000 Germans, of whom we killed 834,000. Meanwhile, Soviet armies of more than 20,000,000 were fighting 5,700,000 Germans at their peak, of whom they killed nearly 2,500,000. America was more efficient, but the Soviet Union had the numbers to keep going.

The danger of this second myth, of the supposed invincibility of the American military, is that it can bring about overconfidence, which leads the country to fight more wars, and for longer than is necessary.

The third myth is that the world learned its lesson. "Never again" became the postwar mantra, typically used to refer to genocide in general and the Holocaust in particular, but it took on other meanings with time. On the 50th anniversary of V.E. Day, Sen. Chris Dodd gave a speech filled with sentences starting with "never again," an indirect acknowledgment of the lesson-myth: "Never again will we face such darkness. Never again will we face the prospect of such global sacrifice. Never again will the forces of freedom be asked to lay down their lives en masse in the name of peace and order."

The danger of the third myth is repeating our mistakes; it may be the most troubling because it precludes progress. If we truly "never again" wanted to ask the forces of freedom to lay down their lives in the name of peace and order, why, then, have we spent over one-third of the time since V.E. Day either in Vietnam or Iraq? That's before accounting for a war in Korea that started in 1950 and never really ended, or any of the dozens of other wars we've waged.

The only thing that changed after V.E. Day is we *never again declared war on anybody*. Congress has the authority under the Constitution to declare war, and the last time it did that was WWII. Not a single war since then has been fought with Constitutional authorization, including the current one being fought in Iraq. So, our legislators authorize funding for a battle they indirectly insist is not a war.

Is that the lesson we learned? Lie to the people? Ignore the Constitution? Fight any war, in any place, at any time? The true lesson our politicians took from V.E. Day wasn't the mythical "never again," but the dictatorial "always and forever." The true lesson we should have taken from V.E. Day is this: The government is not your friend. Don't trust it or let it grow too big.

Ever again.

Originally published on May 9, 2007

What is your value to society? One broadly applicable and fairly objective measure is your lifetime earnings: the total amount of money and other assets that was ever willingly and voluntarily forked over to you.

So Bill Gates doesn't have much value since his salary has always been tiny compared to his wealth from stocks? That would interpret *earnings* too narrowly. Gates' true earnings include cash he received as salary as well as through sales of stock and other assets he's earned, and the current liquidation value of his remaining assets. Thus, he has enormous value to society—you and I, not so much.

Your lifetime earnings are not the same as your current wealth because you may have blown all your earnings on video games or given it away to charity. Warren Buffett's value to society didn't change when he gave away much of his money to charity.

In some arenas, better measures exist. In sports, players can be measured on their contribution to wins. In basketball, a player's value is correlated to points scored, rebounds grabbed, assists handed out, blocks made, etc.

But even in a case such as this, earnings become representative of a person's worth. It's usually accurate to say that more wins means more revenue, and better players are paid more. Even overpaid players who are no longer worth the large contracts they signed earlier are on the receiving end of a willing and voluntary exchange of money.

Sometimes lifetime earnings aren't really the best measure. Posthumous earnings, particularly for artists underappreciated in their lifetime, can dwarf the meager earnings they eked out while alive. Even earnings may not be the proper measure here if a painting continues to increase in price in auction. Neither artist or estate participate in any further price increases, yet the value to society that the artist produced with that one painting is best measured by its current market price.

Furthermore, some people may have near-zero lifetime earnings but have enormous value to society, even if they produced nothing that can be bought or sold. Perhaps they raised their children or helped others or released works into the public domain.

So perhaps it is not easy to define a person's exact value to society, but we have a basic guideline that works fairly well fairly often: the more people are willing to hand over their own assets and wealth in appreciation of a person, the greater his or her value.

What about politicians? Are the best politicians the ones that raise the most money for their campaigns? If not, where does the logic of this measuring break down?

The actions of politicians are of generally two types: those in the best interests of all and those in the best interests of a few. Special interest groups contribute to politicians in the hope that they will bless their constituency with special laws. There are price floors on sugar to benefit the sugar lobby, agricultural subsidies to benefit large farms, tariffs on certain imports to benefit particular domestic industries, and untold earmarks, pork belly projects, tax loopholes, and other favors to benefit the contributors—all on our nickel.

It will be this way so long as elected officials have the power to redistribute money and assets. But it can be minimized. On the federal level, all that is required is a strict limitation on the powers of government officials so that they only focus on issues of national defense, and not on what kind of toilets are illegal or managing farm industry. All that'd be required is some kind of document that spells out what Congress can do, with all other functions relegated to the states or citizens themselves.

Of course, we have such a document. It's called the Constitution. And every elected politician swears to uphold it. Yet very few do.

If all politicians truly acted constitutionally, then their level of campaign contributions might indeed be a good measure of their value to society. Until then, the soaring levels of contributions in many cases only reflect the politician's value to those who would take our money by force.

Originally published on September 5, 2007

Two hundred and thirty-one years ago this Monday, the United States was formed. Two days later, we issued our Declaration of Independence, a day we commemorate with hot dogs and fireworks.

One state declared its own independence before July 4th. One state had the guts and wisdom to reveal the moral basis of government. One state decreed that God inclined people to "set up and establish civil Government for the Protection and Security of their Lives and Properties from the Invasion of wicked Men."

That state, of course, was our state. New York and Pennsylvania were adamantly opposed to independence. Connecticut was the first colony to declare its independence from an oppressive empire. It did so in a heartfelt proclamation issued by Gov. Jonathan Trumbull on June 18, 1776—two and a half weeks before America as a whole followed suit.

Unlike the Declaration of Independence, the Connecticut Proclamation did not hold back sharp words against the British. Trumbull, for whom the town in Fairfield County was named, said they had "degenerated into Tyrants" who "by Fraud or Force betrayed and wrested out of [our] Hands the very Rights and Properties they were appointed to protect and defend."

Thomas Jefferson was upset that Congress removed similarly critical language from the Declaration he authored. "The pusillanimous idea that we had friends in England worth keeping terms with, still haunted the minds of many," he later wrote. "For this reason those passages which conveyed censures on the people of England were struck out, lest they should give them offense."

Today, we Connecticut Yankees are again under the control of a distant government that, by fraud or force, has betrayed and wrested out of our hands the very rights and properties it was appointed to protect and defend.

We are overtaxed. Connecticut citizens pay more in taxes than those of any other state. Our Tax Freedom Day, the day after which we keep what we earn, comes on May 20, the latest in the country. Nearly half the year is spent working for the government rather than our families and selves.

Our properties are confiscated capriciously. They use eminent domain to take the land they want on a basis as corrupt as giving it to someone who they think will pay more taxes. They use asset forfeiture to seize our property; then the burden is on us to prove they were in the wrong. The bar for seizing property is so low that in four out of five asset forfeiture cases no one is even charged with a crime.

Our basic civil and privacy rights are being taken away. Virtually every legislator supported the Patriot Act, at least at some point. The Military Commissions Act was even worse, stripping us of basic defenses, such as the rights to see the evidence against us and to see a judge. National security letters are issued at the drop of a hat to coerce organizations into giving up data on us, and they require no probable cause or even judicial oversight. They often come packaged with a gag order so no one will even know the letter was issued.

They invade foreign countries that pose no imminent danger to us. They enter into what Jefferson called "entangling alliances" that make the U.S. everybody's big brother when a fight comes. They make us far less safe.

The only thing we ask of government is to secure our borders and protect our land and liberty. Instead, they argue over just exactly how much amnesty to give those who enter illegally, and how they can take away more civil liberties from us. They'll make us wear bracelets or inject us with tracking devices. They'll keep a database of retinal scans, fingerprints and DNA, all because they haven't been doing their basic jobs.

The very people we have put in power to protect our property and our rights are stealing those precious things from us.

And what do we do? We don't speak out much. We don't dare call them evil. We don't want to offend.

Thank God we were once the home of citizens who were not afraid to speak up and point out the obvious truth. Thank God they had the courage of morality on their side.

George Washington referred to Trumbull as "Brother Jonathan." That nickname, according to the Connecticut State Library, "came to represent the steady and reliable people of Connecticut." Steady and reliable doesn't mean timid and shy.

Connecticut was considered "the first of patriots" not because we held our tongue for fear of offending our oppressors, but because we weren't afraid of a little fireworks.

Originally published on June 28, 2007

Politicians nowadays of all stripes like to call themselves "fiscal conservatives," meaning they believe in less taxes, less spending, and less debt. Each Republican presidential candidate is clamoring to position himself as "the" fiscal conservative candidate. After the primaries, the Democratic nominee will start to use that term as well.

Democrats use it to try to draw some Republican support. Republicans use the term to appeal to their conservative base. Our own Congressman Christopher Shays has long claimed to be a fiscal conservative. But what does the term mean?

Fiscal conservatism is economic libertarianism; it is the guarding and protecting of economic freedom.

A fiscal conservative basically believes in smaller government control of the economy. The most obvious way to do this is to lower taxes so the government takes less from the people. However, governments are not shy about issuing debt, which is another type of tax. So the best approach is to lower spending overall.

An ideal fiscally conservative government has very low taxes, very low spending, no debt, no deficit, and very few regulatory burdens and restrictions on free trade. We're a long way from there. In the meantime, when candidates for office call themselves fiscal conservatives, they essentially mean they prefer moving in the direction of the ideal, by lowering taxes, spending, and so on.

Candidates spend a lot of time and effort positioning themselves as fiscal conservatives. They do it because it is what the voters want. But what is it about economic freedom that appeals to us so much?

You might even think it should be the opposite, that people should prefer candidates who promise more spending. After all, only a minority of people even pays taxes, so from the point of view of most voters, any government spending is "free."

Historically, that kind of big-government thinking has been the norm since the Great Depression. The Soviet Union seemed to show the world the benefits of a planned economy. Indeed by the 1970s, America had largely become a planned economy as well.

In 1971, President Richard Nixon famously said, "We are all Keynesians now," referring to the policy recommendations of John Maynard Keyes, an economist from the 1920s whose recommendations to tax, borrow and spend influenced most of America's large government programs of the 20th and 21st centuries, including Social Security, welfare, and others. Nixon had taken a 1969 budget surplus and turned it into a deficit. He had imposed wage and price controls. He rationed gas. He was not a fiscal conservative.

Over time, people have begun to see that planned economies are worse than freedom, even if the tax burden does not fall on you. Burdensome regulations and bureaucracy restrict innovation. High taxes, even when only on a minority, take much-needed money out of productive use. High government spending distorts incentives as people begin to compete for more government handouts than more honest business.

The Soviet Union, the darling of Keynesians, collapsed. Government interference in the economy led to inflation. Wage and price controls were seen for what they really are, a way of criminalizing certain economic transactions.

We are all fiscal conservatives now. Very few still believe that an economy planned by politicians can attain anywhere near the wealth of an economy responding to the insights and productivity of millions of Americans.

How much of a fiscal conservative are you? Do you believe taxes, spending and the debt should be much lower and that Americans should be free to go about their business however they wish? Or do you believe that taxes, spending and the debt are basically acceptable at current levels and that we need elected officials to guide the economy in appropriate directions?

The next time you hear someone tell you they are a fiscal conservative, test them with the same questions. See just how far they are willing to go with their beliefs in economic freedom.

Originally published on May 31, 2007

TAX WEIRDOS

Why do people believe in astrology, ESP, ghosts, and the income tax?

There is no established theory yet but there are some common factors, and *Skeptic* magazine publisher Michael Shermer outlines them in his recent book, *Why People Believe in Weird Things*. These factors apply just as easily to the income tax as to aliens, witches, and communing with the dead.

One factor is putting too much weight on anecdotes. Our brains remember coincidences better than non-coincidences but that doesn't make them magical. My favorite story is one told by the physicist Richard Feynman. He was thinking about his sick grandmother when suddenly the telephone rang—and who should it be but a wrong number. His grandmother was fine. She lived for a long time. He committed that incident to memory because similar things happen all the time and we forget them.

Similarly, it's easy to find anecdotes of how tax money is spent on infrastructure or education. But that doesn't mean the income tax is justified. Just think of the states that don't have an income tax, or remember back to when Connecticut didn't have one. We still had bridges and roads and stop signs. The difference? Back then we spend our own money instead of sending it off to a central government, only to have to beg to get some of it back.

Another typical factor is appealing to a long-established tradition or a charismatic leader. Abraham Lincoln instituted an income tax during the Civil War. Funny how wars lead to less liberties for the very people they are being fought to protect; at the time Lincoln imposed his income tax, it was in complete violation of the Constitution.

Another factor can be comfort and fear. We feel comfortable knowing that someone is spending our money on things we probably need. We feel afraid trying to imagine the collapse of civilization that would occur if people stopped paying income taxes. Planes would fall out of the sky. Schools would crumble to the ground. Traffic lights would blink randomly. Your favorite sports team would lose.

A lot of government programs are counter-factual. Take minimum wage laws, intended to promote jobs. How can criminalizing employment create more employment? The income tax is intended to benefit the working class. But the working class are by definition the only ones with income, the only ones who pay taxes. The rich and the poor basically don't work and basically don't pay taxes. How can taxing the working class benefit them in a way they couldn't do themselves?

Most people don't like the income tax or big government. In a recent poll by the liberal organization Democracy Works, an incredible 87 percent of people thought any additional money given to the federal government would be wasted. The majority agreed that government mostly gets in the way of the economy and job growth, and 58 percent actively prefer smaller, more accountable government to one that spends even more money.

A very small minority of people do, however, have either a pseudoscientific or a religious belief in the income tax. It includes liberal Democrats who believe in a centralized power controlling your life and conservative Republicans who believe tax rates should be lowered so that, ironically enough, the overall tax revenue would increase. It doesn't include a single Libertarian.

It's as hard to help income tax lovers as it is to help creationists or Holocaust deniers.

What is the antidote?

Shermer writes that "if there were only one thing… [people] could do to address the overall problem of belief in weird things, constructing a meaningful and satisfying system of morality and meaning would be a good place to start."

Welcome to libertarianism. It exists. It's meaningful, it's satisfying, and, best of all, it's what you believe deep down anyway.

It can be summed up as: Don't hurt others. It is basically the same as the original Golden Rule: what is hateful to you, don't do unto others. In other words: Don't initiate violence.

Freedom is what makes civilizations prosper. It's also the only moral stance, because people are not property, either of each other or of the government. Whoever believes otherwise is a weirdo, to say the least. And what does that make us, the ones who hand over our income to those far-away weirdos on April 15th?

Originally published on April 5, 2007

Politicians love income taxes for the same reason thieves rob banks: that's where the money is. It takes a hardy and independent citizenry to keep its elected officials from dipping their hands into our paychecks, and for hundreds of years, the people of Connecticut stood firm.

In 1971, the Connecticut legislature passed an income tax. One of the lawmakers later recalled that when people would see his legislative license plates they would make obscene gestures at him. We yelled and kicked and screamed so much that the legislature actually repealed the income tax before it even went into effect.

In 1981, with Connecticut facing a budget deficit, the idea was briefly floated again by the legislature. For politicians, an income tax is a panacea, a cure-all, because, after all, their citizens will always earn some kind of income. But again we wouldn't stand for it.

Another decade later, in 1991, the legislature reared once more the ugly head of the income tax. It looked doomed to fail again because new governor Lowell Weicker, a former first selectman of Greenwich and a former Congressman representing Fairfield County, came into office on the back of his pledge to prevent such an atrocity from ever happening.

Then he was inaugurated. Suddenly he fell in love with the income tax.

Weicker became a strong supporter of the tax he had campaigned so strongly against and the happy legislature quickly passed the income tax law.

What did we the people do?

We wouldn't stand for it. After all, no matter how many years go by, we are still a state with a proud streak of libertarianism in our history. An amazing protest of more than fifty thousand people marched on Hartford to demand that we keep our money.

It seemed like history would repeat itself. The legislature once again repealed the very income tax bill it had just passed, just as it had twenty years earlier. The difference this time? The governor.

Weicker vetoed the bill that would have repealed the newly passed income tax.

This was a guy who campaigned against the income tax, changed his mind as soon as he was sworn in, and now vetoed a bill that would have kept us tax-free. He wasn't just failing to keep a promise. He was actively working to sabotage it.

But the citizens, and the legislature, persisted. They moved to override the atrocious veto.

They fell one vote short.

One vote. One legislator. If just one lawmaker in 1981 had changed his mind, we wouldn't have had an income tax in Connecticut for the past 16 years. According to a study last year by the Yankee Institute out of Hartford, in the past decade and a half, because of that missing vote, we went from being one of the least taxed states to one of the most taxed. We lost a greater percentage of 18 to 34 year olds in the 1990s than any other state. We lost a quarter of a million citizens who just couldn't take what was happening to their state. We experienced stagnating employment and lower growth in personal income.

Worst of all, the inflation-adjusted median household income in Connecticut has actually fallen while nationally it has grown.

Thanks to Weicker and our legislators, we have become a poorer state because of the income tax.

Weicker's flip-flop on the issue of taxing income is painful but not uncommon. In fact it seems to be happening to us again.

M. Jodi Rell was an anti-tax state legislator in the early 1990's. After Weicker's term ended, she was elected Lieutenant Governor in 1994 and remained in that post until 2004 when John Rowland resigned as Governor because of corruption charges and she took over the job.

She was elected governor this past November. Last month, she was inaugurated in a huge parade. Like Weicker before her, she fell in love with the income tax.

Rell is now proposing to raise the already burdensome income tax rate in the state. Again, like Weicker, she isn't just failing to reduce your tax burden, she is actively working to increase it.

As famous Hartford resident Mark Twain once said, "History doesn't repeat itself, but it rhymes."

What will the proud libertarian citizens of Connecticut do this time?

Originally published on February 22, 2007

INCOME TAXES ARE BAAAAAAAAD

When I ran for Congress last year, one debate organizer didn't want to include me because I had strong words on my website, for example, calling income taxes a form of theft. They were afraid I'd pepper the debate with salty language—but they soon saw the light and invited me.

It was reported that I had won all of the seven debates against Republican Christopher Shays and Democrat Diane Farrell, but that one was especially memorable. I didn't use the word "theft" but the clarity of my convictions came through and highlighted the similarities of my big-government opponents. The income tax is indeed theft, and the proof is in the changes.

The proof is in the changes?

I heard a famous economist remark about ten years ago that any finite income-tax law will eventually generate zero revenue for the government. What did he mean? People will be drawn to activities that minimize their tax bill. Whatever the deductions or exemptions are, people will gradually have more and more of them until nobody pays any taxes.

The key is that the law has to be stable and finite. Our tax law isn't stable—sometimes changes in interpretation happen right up to April, so you don't even know under what law you worked last year. And it's about as finite as the number of atoms in the universe: countable, but who has the time?

From the time the Constitution was ruined in 1913 by the sixteenth amendment allowing income taxes, until World War II, there were about 500 pages of income tax rules. Say each page of tax law is about 500 words. Those 500 pages would fill three or four full-length novels. So the tax laws for the first twenty years or so were about the size of the *Lord of the Rings* trilogy. It's an enormous chore, and it lacks plot, but it was achievable in a lifetime.

Today, the tax law is more than 50,000 pages—longer than everything you have ever read in your entire life. If you read about 100 words a minute, you'd have to quit your job and read 40 hours per week, for two years, just to know what the law was when you first started. Of course, it changes faster than that.

The government has to change it. If they didn't, we'd eventually stop doing what they penalize us for and start doing what they reward us for. They have to change it so that they just grab the money and run. They introduce an alternative minimum tax (AMT), we don't notice it, and suddenly we owe them more than we planned. Over time, we figure out ways to live without being stung by the AMT, and they just change more rules.

If they didn't change it, we'd adapt and they'd get nothing. So they change the tax law to make it almost random, like a mugger who takes whatever he decides is fair. Taxes with laws that change frequently are more likely to be taxes on people, and more like theft, than taxes with laws that don't change very much. Connecticut's sales taxes, for example, have had only about 30 pages' worth of changes in the past 50 years.

Fair taxes are a lot less like theft. One example is the Fair Tax plan to eliminate all federal taxes and replace them with a single retail sales tax with no exceptions or deductions. There would be pre-paid monthly rebates up to the poverty level so poor people would get cash to offset their expected sales tax requirements, but which they could spend however they want.

The problem is, what mugger would voluntarily stop rifling through your wallet? So the mugger analogy is not the best one. The better one: government treats us like sheep.

Sheep are sheared once a year, in the springtime (April 15). Sheep with long fleeces (sufficiently high incomes) are fleeced more often (quarterly estimated tax payments). Shorn sheep are cold and hungry and rely on handouts from the same people who took their natural insulation.

It's time we stop getting fleeced.

Originally published on April 12, 2007

EVERY DAY SHOULD BE PATRIOT'S DAY

Do you know why you had an extra day to file your taxes this year? It's because in 1775 we fought for our freedom, for less taxes, and for independence. Two hundred and thirty two years later, all we have to show for it is one day? Is that what our patriots died for?

Back then, a three-cent tax on tea got colonists up in arms. They threatened to tar and feather the tax collectors. They threw 45 tons of British tea into Boston Harbor. They risked everything to fight an underdog war for liberty against the world's strongest empire.

Today, every congressmen, senator, state legislator, and even our own governor, feel they can talk about increasing spending and raising taxes with impunity. Those who complain are ridiculed as selfish, greedy, and uncaring. We risk nothing because we can't even imagine true liberty anymore.

Around midnight on April 19, 1775, Paul Revere started riding through the countryside, alerting the people that war was upon them. They lined up and defeated the British at Lexington and Concord. The war had begun.

At midnight on April 18, 2007, Americans breathed a sigh of relief as it was now the longest possible time before they would have to file taxes again. We handed over our privacy, our money, our time, and our dignity. The war was already lost.

Not every state celebrates Patriot's Day. Connecticut doesn't. So why the extension? Because Massachusetts does. Our overlords process our tribute at the IRS building in Andover,

Mass, about half an hour north of Lexington and Concord. Twenty miles and two centuries away from our battle for freedom.

What has happened to our sense of outrage? What true patriot would allow himself to be harvested by his government?

I don't think our natural outrage has been squashed. I don't think our natural yearning for freedom has been destroyed. It's just been pinched and crammed and stuffed into the deepest parts of our hearts, sometimes so deep we forget it is even there—but it's there.

They can play all the word games they want. They can lay all the guilt trips they like. They can tell us about all the wars we have a duty to fight, all the sick we have a duty to heal, all the retired we have a duty to support, and all the poor we have a duty to aid.

We will listen. We will obey. We will commiserate. It is precisely because we value liberty that we are able to be compassionate, and they will use that compassion to pervert our sense of liberty. Let them try. Our moral outrage is a spring. The more they push us down, the stronger we will eventually jump back.

As a people, we haven't changed. The British passed a stamp tax on March 22, 1765. We protested in such a way that few tax collectors were willing to risk their lives to attempt to collect it. The law was repealed a year later.

Connecticut passed an income tax in August, 1991. Legislators who voted for it received death threats. That October, 40,000 people marched on Hartford. Lawmakers rushed outside to announce that they'd repeal the tax in a special session—and less than six months after it was passed, they did.

The difference between then and now? The power of the centralized government. Connecticut's governor vetoed the repeal of the income tax on December 14, 1991. We've been stuck with it ever since.

It's like so much cold water was dumped on us in 1991 that we've become frozen and paralyzed. Let them think that.

The fact is, we're brewing. We are a teapot, building up heat and steam. When we blow our top over taxes, it might look like an over-reaction. Like the patriots we celebrated this past Monday, the tipping point might even be a three cent tax on tea. But we won't be fighting to make it a two cent tax, any more than we would be fighting to gradually lower the marginal tax rate or extend standard deductions. We'll be fighting for principle. We'll be fighting for freedom. For now, we simmer and brew and drink our tea.

Originally published on April 19, 2007

Publicani, or, Dad and Taxes

You never hear people badmouth the income tax anymore. Not even this week, when each of our three hundred thousand Fairfield County households will on average fork over twenty thousand dollars, hundreds of pieces of private and personal information, dozens of otherwise enjoyable hours, and all of our self-respect.

Maybe it's the Stockholm syndrome in action, where, as hostages, we begin to sympathize with our captors who punish and rape us. Whatever the reason, it's nearly impossible to say the income tax is evil. You're either labeled a nut, an insurgent, or a greedy bastard. But is it really crazy to observe that an income tax penalizes effort? Is it really unpatriotic to want your country to be free? Is it greedy to want to keep what's yours?

There are so many things wrong with the income tax—inefficiency, unfairness, counterproductivity—that it's hard to know how best to argue against it. One local author has figured it out.

His name is Zak and he has written a work of fiction called *Publicani*. You've probably heard him on various radio shows over the past week or so, both in English and in Russian. Not everybody can get an interview with him. It helps if you're his son.

Zak Maymin came from the Soviet Union to America with his family, yours truly included, in 1980, and, despite knowing barely any English, earned his Ph.D. in mathematics from MIT that first year. He says he feels he has "come back from the future." He can see which direction our country is going and he knows the end result: "I came from a country that had free health care, free education, complete job security, total political participation of all the people. Most of the people were happy and smiling. Good family values. All of these, that are discussed as goals for America, were implemented in the country I came from and which was an evil empire, as Reagan said. And I don't want America to become an evil empire and that's the major reason why I wrote this book."

Publicani is a family vs. government thriller. "Something that belongs to an individual, nobody can take it from him forcefully," my dad explained. "And if it is taken, the individual has the right to defend himself."

The income tax is never mentioned in the book, but on some level, every word on every page is about it. The original "publicani" were Roman tax farmers during the time of Jesus. "There are, by the way, several chapters in the book where I discuss some religious history and how this principle of individual freedom was traced in other religions and how it is related to Jesus Christ—and where was he, by the way, before he showed up at 30 years old and started doing all these miracles?" *Publicani* answers this question.

But why the income tax? Of all the bad things that could motivate a work of fiction, why this?

"To kill a vampire, you cannot shoot him. You cannot cut his arms and legs. You have to drive a wooden stake through his heart, and it should be wooden and not a silver stick or an iron stick. You have to find one target that is the worst and that is the root of all this evil that is happening in this country, and in my opinion, that's the income tax."

"But why is the income tax the root?"

"It is immoral. It takes by force from others what belongs to them. And it's the clearest example of stealing that government does."

And what is the best possible thing that could happen with this cross between *Enemy of the State*, *Fiddler on the Roof*, and *Atlas Shrugged*, all of which were commercial successes but did not stem the growth of government?

"The problem with the federal income tax is not the government but the fact that people support it. People actually like it. Five percent of the population pays about half the taxes. Other people don't really care. The same way people who were not peasants in Russia and who were not Jews in Germany, they didn't think too much about those things. That's who is the real target of this book. Not the government, but the people who think this way and I hope that maybe I'll be able to change some people in this thinking."

Sold on Amazon.com, etc., the entire text of *Publicani* is also available for free online at publicani.com/book.

Now you can badmouth the income tax all you want.

You are no longer alone.

Originally published on April 17, 2008

Why do we observe Labor Day in September when the rest of the world celebrates it on May 1? And why do we celebrate it with barbecues instead of parades and speeches?

May Day, known as Labour Day everywhere but in America, Canada, Australia, and New Zealand, is a socialist holiday. It commemorates the execution for conspiracy to murder of the organizers of a labor demonstration in Haymarket Square in Chicago in 1886 that got out of hand when an unknown person threw a bomb at a policeman. The "Haymarket martyrs" were the anarchists and socialists leading the rally who had no direct involvement but were found to have "encouraged" the bomber. Four were hanged; on the gallows they sang the Marseillaise, which was then and is now both the anthem of the international revolutionary socialist movement and the French national anthem.

May Day is also called the International Workers Day and is still the biggest day of the year for anarchists, socialists, communists, and organized labor. It is marked by large street demonstrations put together by unions.

May Day and its anarcho-socialist and communist trappings are so reviled in America that every president since Eisenhower in 1958 has proclaimed May 1 both Loyalty Day, a day set aside for "a reaffirmation of loyalty to the United States and for the recognition of the heritage of American freedom," and Law Day, "for the cultivation of the respect for law that is so vital to the democratic way of life." It is a day to celebrate *not* being an anarchist, socialist, or communist. The opposite of what virtually everybody else on the planet is celebrating that day. Little things like this made America one of the last countries to fall into the throes of collectivism. Perhaps we can do one other little thing—rename Labor Day.

We've already moved on from any associations with organized labor. We don't celebrate Labor Day with parades of union workers. We grill meat. We spend time with family. Instead of agitating for political change, we relax. It is a true celebration. And we have Grover Cleveland to thank for it.

President Cleveland was one of our least heralded leaders and arguably the greatest Democratic president of the past 130 years. Cleveland was a libertarian a century before the Libertarian Party was formed. He opposed imperialism, taxes, tariffs, special interests, and the devaluation of America's currency through inflation. He was one of the few and last politicians in America with the integrity to support the gold standard.

But he is better known for being the only president to serve two non-successive terms. Cleveland won in 1884 with support from Democrats and reformist Republicans called "Mugwumps," lost in 1888 due in part to voting fraud, and won again in 1892.

Economics professor Thomas DiLorenzo calls Cleveland the "last good Democrat." He suggests that Cleveland's philosophy is best epitomized in one phrase from his second inaugural address: "The lessons of paternalism ought to be unlearned." Cleveland vetoed every unconstitutional bill that crossed his desk. He railed against any special interests or special favors to any groups for any reason. In foreign policy, he cited Washington and Jefferson in avoiding entangling alliances. He was a good president—twice.

Haymarket happened in his first term. Socialists and labor organizers the world over tried to use the tragedy to bolster their desire for a May 1 labor holiday. Cleveland feared that a national labor holiday coinciding with the anniversary of the riots would strengthen the socialist movement. The Knights of Labor, a smaller labor group that wasn't involved with the riots, had organized labor parades for several years in September. Cleveland adopted their position and put Labor Day on the calendar. The holiday called for parades to exhibit "the strength and esprit de corps of the trade and labor organizations," but Americans transformed it into a day of fun.

May Day is a commemoration of death and an ode to planned economies and big government. The day and the holiday we celebrate the first Monday of every September is a celebration of life, family, spontaneity; it has become a libertarian holiday.

Why not make it official? Let's rename it Grover Cleveland Day in honor of the man who has given us an extra day of summer every year.

Originally published on August 30, 2007

If you want proof that government is slow, irrelevant and counterproductive, you can just think back to the Monday two weeks ago when you didn't have to work. We call it President's Day, and we think we're celebrating the birthdays of both George Washington and Abraham Lincoln.

But we're not.

Here in Connecticut, we had already celebrated Lincoln's birthday the previous Monday. It was only a state holiday, of course, and so most people worked.

Why do people typically work on state holidays but not on federal holidays? Both types of holidays are mandatory only for government employees anyway.

The answer is banks. Banks usually observe federal holidays but not state holidays. When banks are closed, companies relying on cash business are likely to be closed. Their vendors and clients are then likely to be closed as well. And it snowballs.

But why do banks observe federal holidays but not state ones? It's because the Federal Reserve Banks are closed. Federal holidays are Fed holidays and Fed holidays are bank holidays.

But wait! I thought the Fed was something complicated and distant. Perhaps a system of regional divisions providing local oversight, or a collection of economists poring over data to determine optimal interest rates, or a unified location for money exchange—all things that could be done without or through alternatives for a day.

It's much simpler. The Fed is a government-controlled monopolistic central bank.

All banks do business with the Fed. They have no choice. If you wanted to lend and borrow money and take deposits from people, you would have to do business with the Fed as well. If you don't, you will be punished. By the feds.

We don't work on federal holidays because the central bank we are forced to use is closed and we are not allowed to create alternatives. If the Fed were a private company, even a private monopoly, anybody could create a competitor that stayed open year-round. But when it's a government monopoly enforced by laws and guns, your hands are tied. It doesn't sound like something George Washington would be particularly proud of, does it?

Washington was born Friday, Feb. 22, 1732. Yet we celebrate President's Day on the third Monday of every February, which by definition can never fall later than Feb. 21. Yes, a federal law aiming to commemorate a birthday is guaranteed to never commemorate it on the right day. Yes, government is counterproductive.

Technically, Washington was born on Feb. 11. What happened? Pregnant women need not fear: it was not an 11-day delivery. In 1751, Britain passed a law to move to the Gregorian calendar, the one we use today, to fix a leap-year flaw that had resulted in about a 10-day difference. According to the new British law, the day after Wednesday, Sept. 2, 1752 would be Thursday, Sept. 14, 1752. And so it was.

It's called the Gregorian calendar because it was adopted by Pope Gregory XIII in 1582. So why did it take 169 years for Britain and the American colonies to adopt it? You think time zones are difficult: before the British change, we were off by 11 days from all of continental Europe. Parisians celebrated the New Year 11 days before Londoners. (Actually, for government purposes it was even more than that: under the old calendar the year started March 15 for legal purposes, not Jan. 1.)

Yes, government is slow. And it's not just the British. Connecticut took 149 years to ratify the Bill of Rights!

So why the long British delay? Because the Protestant Reformation had just begun in the 16th century and the Protestant state of Britain out of principle didn't want to be seen agreeing with any papal decree. Do you think irrational stubbornness doesn't exist in our current government?

And that's the history of President's Day—except for one small thing: It's not actually called President's Day. The holiday is and always has been legally known as Washington's Birthday. It's just not what we the people call it in our everyday lives. Yes, government, at its best, when it's not punishing people, is irrelevant. If only the Fed were as irrelevant.

The last chapter on your February day off came six months before 9/11. A bill in the House would have required all federal entities and officials to refer to the holiday only as "Washington's Birthday" and by no other name.

It died in subcommittee.

Originally published on March 1, 2007

The Cheese of Justice: The Libertarian Leap Year

You may think that this Friday, Feb. 29th, is just a trick to bring the average days per year closer to the 365.25 days that it takes to revolve around the sun. But it may well be an unheralded libertarian festival.

Did you think it takes exactly 365 days for the Earth to do a solar loop? You're not alone—so did the ancient Egyptians. Although to be fair (to the Egyptians, not to you), they used a 365-day calendar because that happened to be the regular flooding schedule of the Nile river. (What's your excuse?) It resulted in their traditional summer months eventually becoming winter months before cycling back, all over a period of many hundreds of years.

Nevertheless, the Egyptian calendar was still one of the best. It had replaced at least partially the lunar calendar that they had experimented with before, and which still persists. The Hebrew calendar, the Chinese calendar, the Hindu calendar, and the Islamic calendar are all lunar even today.

How can those calendars survive if they are so wrong? The answer is leap months. All lunar calendars are so off, usually by about ten days a year, that they have to add a whole new month every two to three years.

There is one exception: The Islamic calendar does not have leap months. It is forbidden in the Koran. Instead, it simply starts eleven days earlier relative to our regular years.

(About three times a century, a Muslim year falls entirely within a regular year. Coincidentally, it's happening this year:

What we know as 2008 incorporates the entirety of the Muslim year 1429.)

So what's a "regular" year? Technically, it's a Gregorian year, or sometimes a Julian year. Pope Gregory XIII made a mild modification in 1582 to a calendar that Julius Caesar had implemented in 45 BCE.

What did Caesar do two thousand years ago that was so stunningly impressive that it remained the standard calendar for virtually the entire world for so long?

And why did he do it?

Before Caesar's change, Rome was also on a lunar calendar. They had leap months that should have been followed on a fairly rigid schedule, much like the Hebrew, Chinese, and Hindu calendar do today, but the final decision was made by bureaucrats and politicians. As you might expect, they didn't always do what was right, but let politics interfere.

How arbitrary were the human-directed leap months? To cite Wikipedia, "They usually occurred every second or third year, but were sometimes omitted for much longer, and occasionally occurred in two consecutive years."

In times of war, leap months were sometimes entirely forgotten or done less frequently than needed to keep the year close to seasonal. This is not because it was unimportant. Quite the opposite: People desperately needed an accurate and consistent calendar. The last, failing years of the human-directed lunar calendar were known as the "years of confusion."

Here's where Caesar got libertarian. He thought that smaller government could be more stable and less confusing. So he decided to set it and forget it; make an algorithm, open-source it, and get the human element out of the way. He added a day or two to some of the lunar months Rome had been using. We still use these exact same months today.

That first step brought the total number of days per year up from 355 to 365. That's already pretty close! But he went one better than the ancient Egyptians. He added a single leap day, instead of an entire leap month, occurring exactly every four years.

That's it. One more function of government shut down, and the people were better off.

(Pope Gregory's contribution was to further adjust the leap day calculations with wrinkles for years divisible by 100. It turns out that the true year length is closer to 365.24 than 365.25. But it took about one and a half thousand years for it to make a significant difference.)

How many of our government functions are being neglected, just like leap months were, now that we are in a time of war? Education. Health care. Elderly benefits. Poverty aid. Even veterans are getting short shrift.

Perhaps it's time we made a Caesar's salad (named for an entirely different Caesar, mind you) out of our bloated government. Toss away the tomatoes and onions and other extras that we can each add to our salad to our own individual taste. Leave just the lettuce of a national defense, the cheese of justice, and the sauce of freedom. And please bring the salty anchovies of boring presidential primaries on the side. Some of us are allergic.

Originally published on February 28, 2008

Like you, I set my clocks forward nearly a month earlier than usual this year. The reason? A new 551-page law passed by Congress in 2005.

The relevant section takes up just the middle third of page 23, but caused a substantial interference in the lives of Americans. Known as the "Y2K7 Bug" because lots of electronic devices did not update correctly, it'll hit us again in a week or so when our gizmos automatically adjust for what they think ought to be daylight savings time.

We'll face similar problems in November as the change happens one week later than usual. People will again miss appointments. Various medical devices may malfunction, and you'll never know until it's too late. All this trouble from just 17 lines of a single 551-page law. Makes you wonder how much trouble is on the other 500 pages.

Is daylight savings time even a good idea? The myth I remember from public school is that it's good for farmers. Nothing could be further from the truth. Farmers *hate* daylight savings time. If you used to milk your cow at five with pickup scheduled for seven, now you have to milk her at six, giving you *less* time to get to market.

The history of daylight savings time began 100 ago when the great-great-grandfather of Coldplay lead singer Chris Martin came up with the idea. Martin's 2003 megahit "Clocks" even sounds like a song that's against daylight savings. Its first line: "Lights go out and I can't be saved."

It took a world war for the idea to become law, as Britain tried to conserve coal during WWI. It came to America as a temporary measure and was soon repealed—but by then government had created a mess.

In 1920s Ridgefield, for example, half the businesses were on standard time and half were on advanced time.

After WWII, and more temporary federal programs, the mess got even worse. One infamous 35-mile stretch of highway went through *seven* time zones. "Clocks" again: "Confusion that never stops\the closing walls and ticking clocks." Martin, who wrote the lyric, says he doesn't know where it came from. But now we know.

Government eventually stepped in to "fix" the very mess it had created. And daylight savings time was born.

What's the alternative to federally mandated clock tinkering? How about letting people live on whatever schedule they like? Open businesses early or late as they wish. Plenty of businesses have summer hours. It's basically the same idea. The only argument I can see for federal laws is to control when federal offices are open, and given how intrusive government has become, that would then dictate when free businesses are open.

But it turns out that's a myth too! In 1967, Michigan petitioners passed a referendum that temporarily prohibited daylight savings time. What did federal offices do? According to an article in *Time* from that year, they "shifted obediently, then moved their office hours up one hour to cancel out the off-phase effect."

The government tinkering never stops. You think this is the first time someone had the bright idea of extending daylight savings time? In 1974, Richard Nixon made it last for 15 months.

Yes, government is just that stupid.

At the end of the day (whenever that is by current federal law), I don't care what time it is, as long as I'm not late for lunch. But I don't like being forced to pay for protection, mafia-style, from a problem the putative protector perpetrated.

Next time you hear someone explain how the Federal Reserve solved the banking crisis, how federal welfare ended the Great Depression, or how the Homeland Security won the war on terror, think of daylight savings time.

Were the problems caused by the government in the first place? (Yes, yes, and yes.) Would the problems go away if they just let people be free? (Yes, yes, and yes.) If the government solution is so divinely perfect, why do they keep changing it? (Exactly!)

Originally published on March 22, 2007

The following is attributed to Alexander Tytler:

> *The average age of the world's greatest civilizations from the beginning of history has been about 200 years. During those 200 years, these nations always progressed through the following sequence:*
>
> - *From bondage to spiritual faith;*
> - *From spiritual faith to great courage;*
> - *From courage to liberty;*
> - *From liberty to abundance;*
> - *From abundance to complacency;*
> - *From complacency to apathy;*
> - *From apathy to dependence;*
> - *From dependence back into bondage.*

Why do free countries tend to become less free with time? The quote above offers one famous but depressing view, the idea being that the majority eventually learns to vote for itself the property of the minority.

It's not just a theoretical point. It's happening to us right now. More than half of American households pay no income tax at all: the voting majority. A mere 25 percent of Americans pay more than two-thirds of the total income tax: these are the minority whose property is being taken away.

Who are these unfortunate minorities? The typical Fairfield County resident. The income level associated with the top 25 percent of tax payers is $60,000. The median household income in the county is $65,000.

Stopping the majority from awarding itself your property is the key to freedom. It's why our founding fathers rejected unlimited democracies in favor of a republic that, in principle, could never take away your property by a popular vote. The Constitution explicitly forbade an income tax and set clear and firm limits on the power of Congress and the White House.

Being a Congressman should be the easiest job in the world. Virtually all bills proposed nowadays are unconstitutional, making your vote obvious. It's why I ran for Congress last year: I knew I could get the job done. But finding representatives who actually honor their inaugural oath to uphold the Constitution is almost impossible. The classic counterexample is Ron Paul of Texas, a physician who has earned the nickname "Dr. No" by frequently being the lone voice of opposition to unconstitutional bills.

Do we lose freedoms because we have bad presidents? What if a person like Paul were President? Paul has announced he is running in the Republican primary, so it's not impossible. And he's the kind of Republican you would like: consistently opposed to the Iraq war, opposed to taxes, and opposed to government invasion of your privacy.

He's almost like Ronald Reagan.

Reagan was the most libertarian-sounding American president of the past 150 years. We can argue over whether he implemented what he said, but his speeches and principles were always about the problems of government, the evils of tyranny, and the "collective genius and common sense" of millions of free Americans.

In fact, it is Reagan who may have been the first person to attribute the democracy quote to Tytler, back in 1964. The quote was well-known before then, but nobody knew who said it, and there's no evidence that Tytler ever did.

I used to think that Reagan was an anomaly, and the exception that proved the rule: the kind of people who run for office and win tend to be the kind of people who crave power. To such people, Constitutional limits mean nothing. These are the kinds of people who vote for higher taxes, more war, less privacy.

I thought that it was this selection bias of power-hungry lawmakers that was the mechanism by which our freedoms erode. The quote attributed to Tytler explained the process, and the selection bias provided the means. But where's the catalyst?

I now think it is tragedies. Tragedies take away our freedoms. Tragedies are rare but heart-stopping events. When tragedy strikes, we run like a scared child to the nearest source of power we can, and cling to it.

Five and a half years ago, Richard Reid boarded a flight from Paris to Miami and tried to detonate explosives in his shoes. Now we all walk in socks on dirty airport carpets, spreading germs and getting sick.

Last year, 24 people were arrested, and 16 eventually charged, with trying to detonate liquid explosives. Now we all measure our shampoos and perfumes by the ounce.

Two weeks ago, an English major at Virginia Tech shot and killed 32 people, injuring 29 others, before committing suicide. The *New York Times* immediately called for more gun control laws.

It's a natural, instinctive reaction. Never mind that guns were already banned at Virginia Tech. Never mind that another deadly shooting four years ago and a hundred miles to the west was stopped by students who ran to their cars to get their own guns. Never mind that seven years before that, an assistant principal in Mississippi got a handgun from his car to successfully stop a shooter. Never mind that reportedly all school shootings over the past decade that ended abruptly were stopped because a potential victim had a gun.

In times of tragedy, logic gets thrown out the window. It's an empirical fact that gun-control laws kill, because they are effectively victim-disarmament laws.

Criminals will always get guns, just as they can always move explosives from their shoes to their crotch, or combine carry-on liquids from several passengers. But we are left to suffer the counterproductive laws that limit our freedom.

There is no natural antidote to knee-jerk laws passed after tragedies. When times are great, people do not rush their legislatures to repeal earlier invasive laws. And so totalitarianism builds.

This month's massacre is not a spark for more debate on gun control laws. That debate is pointless: gun ownership is moral and effective. You have the right to protect yourself, period. Additionally, when citizens are free to own guns, there are fewer victims.

The real lesson here should be: How can we make government honor its limits? How can we get our representatives to start saying, "No, we can't do that, it's unconstitutional?"

Tragedies are scary enough. We shouldn't have to endure the insult of less freedom on top of the injury itself.

Originally published on April 26, 2007

Do you have rights that the government protects for you, or do you have privileges that the government grants you?

Last week, *Weekly* editor Tom Gogola called for a repeal to the Second Amendment, partially in response to my column describing how tragedies tend to lead to totalitarianism.

He posed two arguments: one, that the right being protected by the amendment is the unnecessary right to overthrow our government, and two, that gun ownership ought to be a privilege, not a right. Which is it?

The Bill of Rights was originally proposed to clarify that the federal government was to be limited in its powers. The first ten amendments made it painfully obvious that the government can not and will not infringe on our most sacred rights, such as freedom of speech, due process, self defense, and so on. Could the list itself have been misinterpreted as all-encompassing, so that if a right was not mentioned, it was implicitly something government could control? No. The last two amendments specified that any rights not mentioned belong to the states or the people, not to the federal government.

Today, the people of Connecticut tend to favor gun control laws, and could possibly be bullied into an outright repeal of the Second Amendment by editors of weekly newspapers. Back in 1789, Connecticut refused to ratify the Bill of Rights. Was it because we did not like the Second Amendment even then?

On the contrary. Connecticut refused to ratify because it felt the Bill of Rights was unnecessary. *Of course* people can arm themselves. *Of course* they can worship as they wish. *Of course* rights exist first and governments are created to protect them.

The Bill of Rights, of course, passed anyway.

In 1939, embarrassed as its 150th anniversary was approaching, Connecticut finally ratified the Bill of Rights, becoming the last state to do so, a century and a half late, and 68 years to the day before Gogola called for its partial repeal. At the time, with a world war in the works, Americans remained fiercely loyal to the Bill of Rights and to liberty, at a time when totalitarianism seemed to be sweeping the globe.

If we were to adopt a new Constitution today, it almost surely would not have gun rights. It would probably look less like the U.S. Bill of Rights and more like the U.N. Declaration of Human Rights. What's the difference?

The U.S. Bill of Rights takes pains to clarify that it simply protects the most important rights and freedoms, and that the list "shall not be construed to deny or disparage others retained by the people."

Taking the opposite approach, the U.N. document asserts that even those rights and freedoms it specifically lists may "in no case be exercised contrary to the purposes and principles of the United Nations." Under the U.N.'s guidelines, you'd never read this article. I'd never be able to write it.

Gun control advocates and Second Amendment repealers want the U.N. approach. We, the unwashed masses, would be told what we can do and when and how we can do it. Our lives would amount to begging for more privileges. Not on my watch.

Governments are formed for one of two reasons: to oppress or to protect. Prior to America, virtually all governments oppressed their citizens. The people were an asset to be tamed and used like beasts. But we were unique. We were a people who organized government for our own use, to protect our rights. Essentially, we established qualified bodyguards.

And you can fire the bodyguard: Yes, you do have the right—the duty—to overthrow the government when it becomes oppressive or incapable of protecting you. And though a bodyguard is nice to have, you're never prevented from defending yourself. If someone sneaks past the bodyguard, or he isn't very good, it's up to you to protect your life.

There are higher things involved here than words on a page. No matter what any Constitution says, you have the right to defend yourself against violence. You know that; you can feel that in your heart. You know that you can use your fists. You can use a stick. You can throw rocks. You can fashion a slingshot. You can shoot a gun. Whatever the attacker has, you can have more.

When someone comes to take away your natural, inalienable, pre-existing right to defend yourself, even if like the U.N. they offer you "free" education and health care, even if they assure you that no one else will be able to defend themselves either, you will know that you have been tamed. You will know that you are no longer a citizen of a free country, but the property of an oppressive one. Fight back now, before it's too late; before your right to bear arms is replaced by bare arms.

Originally published on May 3, 2007

The Supreme Court is deciding whether a complete ban on all handguns in Washington, D.C. violates the second amendment of the Constitution, which says that "the right of the people to keep and bear Arms shall not be infringed."

You might think, if you have even passing familiarity with the word "infringe," that the answer is obvious. And indeed early reports indicate the Supremes will decide that you do, in fact, have an individual right to bear arms.

Why was there any doubt? For two reasons, or rather, one motivation and one excuse. The motivation was simply to make the government larger and with more power over your life. The excuse has been the first part of the second amendment, which begins with the clause, "A well regulated Militia, being necessary to the security of a free State..." Does that mean that the right to guns extends only to members of a militia? Or only in circumstances when a militia is necessary to our security?

There is no real argument here. That clause does not modify the right nor place restrictions on it. It is like the preamble to a document, contract, or even the Constitution itself. By analogy, if we are no longer interested in forming a more perfect union, does the entire Constitution cease to matter?

This is the silly decoy argument that the Supreme Court appears ready to stamp out. They will almost surely say that the second amendment protects an individual's right to bear arms, militia or no militia.

That might seem like a victory for freedom, but the court won't stop there. They have to decide whether the handgun ban in D.C. is constitutional or not and how to decide what restrictions on weapons are legit. Safety locks? Individually-identified bullets? Waiting periods? Assault-weapon bans?

No one knows how they will decide yet. But the readers of the Weekly deserve to know ahead of time, so I'll tell you: they'll use the reasonable weasel. They'll say any law has to be "reasonable."

It's a trap. Whenever a politician says, "Let's be reasonable," the ghosts of the founding fathers reach for their guns.

Who decides what is reasonable? If you allow the government to decide what is a reasonable violation of your rights, then you no longer have unalienable rights to be protected by your elected officials, you have privileges granted to you by your prison warden.

Should we allow warrantless wiretapping as a reasonable defense against terrorism? How about a national ID card and restrictions on employers as a reasonable step against illegal immigration? Putting a million innocent people on a do-not-fly list? Imprisoning one in every one hundred Americans? Torture?

In my 2006 debate against Republican congressman Christopher Shays and Democratic challenger Diane Farrell, the issue of gun rights came up, and I pointed out that the second amendment prohibits any congressman from infringing even slightly on the right to bear arms. The clip is available on YouTube. I challenged each of them, both of whom support sweeping legislation against gun rights, to point to any area of the Constitution that authorizes them to do so. Of course, neither did. Shays said in essence that he believes it is up to him to determine what are "reasonable" restrictions, like trigger locks, etc.

But it's not. The text of the Constitution is clear. "Shall not be infringed" does not mean "shall not be infringed unless the person doing the infringing thinks it's okay."

There is a well-established concept of reasonableness used in the law, and that is the reasonable person standard. This is how courts determine, for example, whether someone was negligent. They will ask if you exercised the standard of care that a reasonable person would. In this case, a reasonable person is someone like you, but who exercises due care in a calm and collected way.

It is often up to the jury to decide if an act was reasonable or not. Note the difference with politicians: the twelve jurors have no other stake in the outcome, no lobbyists pushing one way or another, and no need to appeal to large groups of people to earn their vote later. They vote their consciences, once, and go home. And the decision can differ from case to case.

But when the government gets involved, and uses the reasonable weasel, it is a trap. Did you think I was merely guessing what the founding fathers think about the situation? Search for REASON in the main text of the Constitution; it appears seven times—as part of TREASON.

Originally published on March 27, 2008

What are you in for? "I sent spam to kids."

You monster!

Ever wonder why America has more people in jail than any other country, including China? Or why the United States has the highest incarceration rate of any country on earth? Here's why: We ignore our Constitution and pass stupid laws.

Here's the most recent example: A new Connecticut proposal would create a do-not-call list for children, including their cellphone numbers and e-mail addresses. Companies looking to spam your kids would have to scrub their databases by submitting what they have to the registry maintainers, who would then flag the offending entries. It's a proposal that epitomizes how laws get proposed and passed nowadays. I will reveal the algorithm to you.

First, start with the children. Everyone wants to protect the children. You can try to substitute animals, minorities, the working poor, or the handicapped, though it's not as surefire.

Next, find some threat to them. Novices look for real threats of harm, like gang violence or car accidents. Professional lawmakers are not so limited. For them, imagined threats are just as good, like low self-esteem or going to hell if they hear about Darwin.

Now the fun part: thinking up "good ideas." Wouldn't it be a "good idea" to get rid of guns? Make cars drive slower? Have teachers focus on self-esteem? Teach kids alternative theories to evolution?

The distance from "good idea" to "law proposal" is thinner than a knife edge. It's literally nothing more than applying force to get your desire result. Let's make guns illegal! Impose speed limits! Leave no child behind! Authorize creationism in the curriculum!

There is only one thing standing in the way of the proposal becoming actual law: How many people would be immediately and directly affected by it? I believe there's a magic number involved here: If fewer than 20 percent of the people are affected, the proposal has a strong chance to become law, no matter how inane. But if more than 20 percent are affected, it's not likely to happen.

Why 20 percent? Because people vote. Even if the law proposed is not on a referendum, and even if there is no election this year, eventually, in the long run, people make their voices felt, one way or another. Why is the magic number as small as one in five? Because typically only half the people vote anyway. So of the 50 percent that vote, you need the support of more than half of them. Plus, most of the immediately and directly affected people are more likely to vote, so you need a cushion for that.

How does this apply to our examples? In most times and places, fewer than one in five own guns, so laws regulating gun ownership are quick to pass, even if they are unconstitutional. But far more people drive cars, so it's much harder to pass onerous driving restrictions.

In the latest example, we start, as always, with the poor, innocent, defenseless children. You don't want them stalked by predators and child molesters, do you? What kind of heartless person are you? Plus, you don't want greedy marketers finding them and trying to push video games and blue jeans on them. So: wouldn't it be a good idea to make it illegal for marketers to call children?

Oh, wait. That would mean virtually everybody is immediately and directly affected.

How about making it optional, so that parents can add their children's info to the registry, but are not obligated to?

There you go: that's less than 20 percent. The law is all but on the books.

Never mind that all taxpayers will have to pay the cost of prosecuting, jailing and rehabilitating those pesky marketers who flout the law and call or e-mail kids anyway.

Never mind that this is the sort of thing a voluntary, private organization can and should do. Never mind that everybody already has caller-id and spam filters.

And certainly never mind that the government is too big already precisely because of such thinking.

No, it's a "good idea" and so we have to lose a little bit more freedom. A little here, a little there, none of which is worth fighting over. It's how we got to where we are today, paying half as much to the government as we take home for ourselves, and having 25 percent of all the world's prisoners despite having only 5 percent of the world's population.

Originally published on January 5, 2007

WINGING IT

Take off your shoes, toss out your cologne, and open your wallet. No, that's not a pickup line. It's what our well-paid government has come up with to try to prevent the same things that didn't happen before from not happening again in the exact same way.

Richard Reid didn't blow up a plane by lighting plastic explosives hidden in his shoes.

Twenty-five people arrested in London last year didn't blow up any planes by using liquid explosives.

But now all shoes must be removed, even flip-flops and sandals. All liquids must be thrown out or put into checked baggage, even perfume, deodorant, shampoo and hairspray. And you have to show a government-issued and unexpired ID to earn the privilege of being X-rayed, and keep your boarding pass out for them to check it and check it again.

These rules assume terrorists are utterly unimaginative and Americans are utterly terrified. Terrorists, the deep thinking presumably goes, who were willing to blow themselves up on a plane by carrying plastic explosives in their shoes, would never, ever put them in their pants. That stuff itches! And Americans would never dare complain about security measures. Security! Safety! Be afraid! Now get back in line!

Why do we let these regulations ruin our summer vacations and delay our friends and family from flying back home to visit? These rules do absolutely nothing to stop future terrorist attacks and they cost us all money, energy, and time.

How can a terrorist get around them? Put explosives in your underwear. Split up the liquids into several containers brought on board by multiple passengers. Get some fake IDs. Copy an old boarding pass and change some info on it. This isn't rocket science. It's trivially obvious.

How much do these rules cost us? Nearly seven hundred million passengers fly each year. Say 20 percent used to never check any luggage. That sped up the luggage handling of the remaining passengers and lowered ticket costs because of the reduced labor. But let's just look at the new costs now imposed on just these people. With the new regulations, maybe about half of them now check some baggage. They easily spend an extra fifteen minutes waiting for their bags. That's more than a million man-hours wasted each month.

None of this counts the amount of printing the government did to put informative posters everywhere. Or what's worse, the increased funding they will repeatedly ask for when they point to this initiative as one of their biggest successes.

With the security checks, baggage checks, and sanity checks, it's getting to be that taking a train or a bus from around here to Boston or D.C. may be faster than flying.

Where else does government make things worse for regular people without stopping criminals at all? Gun regulations. Criminals will always be able to get guns, but potential victims are unable to defend themselves without going through massive red tape and tossing out their privacy rights.

It's not like the problem is particularly hard to solve. The free market solves easy stuff like transportation security for breakfast. It then has a healthy lunch on corporate fraud and a tasty dinner on environmental protections. (It likes to save education for dessert.) The free market is a gourmand of solutions but government regulations are all too often poisonous.

What's one easy way to provide security? Well, there are three main risks: hijacking, exploding, and torpedoing. Hijacking can be prevented with sealed cockpit doors for the duration of the flight, undercover agents with guns, and guns in the cockpit for the pilots. Using an airplane to crash into a building, is no more or less preventable than it was before. Terrorists can always buy a small plane. So what about exploding?

The free market isn't just one guy making whimsical decisions. It's millions of people each offering you what they think you want. When they're right, they make money. You're willing to make some kind of trade-offs between risk and convenience: you drive a car, you fly a plane, you eat fatty foods. Some people may have different preferences. Some prefer convenience a lot more, some prefer safety, just like some prefer vegetables and others prefer meat.

What does the free market do? It offers a choice!

Different airlines could offer different amount of security. Some of us might choose far more security, and far more reasonably implemented than just stripping us of shoes, liquids, dignity, and pride. Some of us might prefer less security with fewer delays. Those of willing to pay for the extra security with longer wait times and higher ticket prices will get what we want. And so will those of us who just want to fly home.

No IDs? Only one check of your boarding pass instead of three? It's hard to imagine being able to travel with a large quantity of people at a fast speed without having to prove your legal existence many times over. How can that possibly happen? Seems to work fine for trains, subways, and busses.

Wouldn't it be nice to live in a world where you could legally keep your shoes on while traveling?

Originally published on July 5, 2007

Why do we tip waitresses but not stewardesses? Why do we tip taxi drivers but not teachers, doctors or lawyers?

The answer: unions. Flight attendants and teachers are unionized; waitstaff and cabbies are not. Without unions, we pay people what they are personally worth, not what the average person in their industry is worth. You tip your masseuse because she is your masseuse (or masseur if you prefer a monsieur) and you want to reward her personally.

Unions exist to protect the average salary. Their function is to increase the pay of their worst performing members at the double expense of underpaying their best performing members and preventing new entrants. The only way they can survive is to limit the number of newcomers to just enough to replace retirees. If too many people are suddenly willing to teach or practice law, the average salary of a teacher or lawyer drops. Even if the new workers are much better workers and could earn more without the union, if the overall average drops, the union has failed.

The clearest example is the NBA. Superstars earn the maximum allowable contract and are, all things considered, great bargains for owners. Young or lousy players are guaranteed their salary regardless of performance, and new entrants are limited by age restrictions and the draft process.

Did you know that doctors and lawyers are basically unionized too? It may not seem like it. After all, unlike public school teachers or flight attendants, their salary is negotiable and they compete against each other. But they are often members of the AMA and the Bar Association. These organizations wield even more influence than a typical union because they are virtually always used by states to determine the legal ability of people to enter a profession.

At first blush that seems like a good thing. Why not protect innocent American consumers from the fraud and incompetence that an unqualified professional could bring?

Because it limits the consumer's choice, that's why.

Consider the jobs that are halfway between unionized and non-unionized, jobs that have high hurdles to obtain legal licenses. For example, not everybody can be an electrician. It's dangerous! It some states, it's harder to get an electrician's license than in others. You might expect those states to be much safer, electrically speaking. You might expect the average number of accidental electrocutions, for instance, to be far lower in the more rigid states. Turns out it's the exact opposite. The more rigid the rules, the more accidental shocks. Why?

Licensing restrictions limit the total number of electricians. But people need the services of electricians, so their prices go up. At the higher price, you are more likely to try to fix the problem yourself and save the money. Zap!

If there were no licensing restrictions at all, you could choose an electrician based on experience and expertise. You would be able to make a tradeoff between what you can afford and the quality you can buy, but licensing restrictions cut off the smooth transition and make it an all-or-nothing game.

Minimum wage laws work the same way. At best, they increase the average salary—at best. But, of course, they reduce the amount of people who work. They don't allow a smooth transition from zero dollars per hour up to ten dollars per hour in terms of the quality of person you can hire. And because American citizens who earn below minimum wage can report their employers and receive the "missing" back pay, all those illegal jobs go to undocumented workers and other people who do not have the legal standing to report their employers.

Here's a tip from me to you: abolish minimum wage laws and the flood of illegal immigration would slow down to a trickle. Americans would no longer be legally barred from taking those jobs, and they would take them. The demand for illegal employees would evaporate.

Here's another tip: remove licensing restrictions. Why should hair stylists have to study for an exam before they can braid your hair? Why should single moms have to get a degree in education and a charter for a private school before they are allowed to teach or care for their local neighborhood kids?

So what's your tip for more freedom and less government?

Originally published on July 12, 2007

Do you remember where you were when the stock market crashed on Monday, October 19, 1987, plummeting more than 20 percent in a single day? What lessons have we learned two decades later? Can this sort of thing ever happen again?

I was 12 at the time, sitting in my eighth grade Social Studies class. When the clock ticked 9:32 a.m., the assistant principal poked his head in the room and pulled me out. This was well before cellphones and the internet and any other way of communicating other than calling the school with a message.

When I got to the principal's office, he relayed the news from my parents: my brother Allan had been born fifteen minutes earlier. I didn't know or care that the market had crashed until years later. How's that for perspective?

A big deal was made out of the crash at the time and retrospectives every decade make it seem like it was the end of the world. Statistically, indeed, it was extraordinary.

The principal model of stock market movements is that of a random walk, which for historical reasons is always described as a drunken man stumbling away from a lamp post. During each interval, he lurches forward either to his left or his right. The size of his steps are on average three feet but sometimes he takes a smaller step, sometimes he takes a larger one.

That's a pretty good model of stock prices, which go either up or down, often about one percent a day, but sometimes less and sometimes more. But what happened on October 19, 1987, when the market moved more than 20 percent in a single day is the equivalent of the drunk somehow stumbling 60 feet, about half the length of an Olympic size swimming pool, in a single bound.

What's more is that later that week the market corrected upwards almost as violently. Even excluding Monday, that week was one of the most volatile in Wall Street history.

To this day, nobody really knows what happened. Some blamed and continue to blame arbitrageurs and so-called "program trading," orders placed by computer that tend to sell when the market falls, thus exacerbating any random fluctuations. It's like little kids running around the drunk: when he lurches left, they push him a little more to the left, making him stumble even more in the same direction.

Still it's hard to imagine those kids causing such a large leap purely randomly. Economist Richard Roll makes a persuasive case that program trading was not the culprit at all. Program trading was primarily an American phenomenon, he says, and the crash actually began in Hong Kong, moved to Europe, and arrived in the U.S. that Monday morning.

Another way of thinking about this is to consider Brownian motion, the phenomenon that occurs when you put small things in a liquid. The example here is pollen particles in water. For some reason, the pollen starts to fidget around. Each little water molecule is so small relative to the pollen that it can't possibly budge it. The mystery is solved when you realize there are thousands of little molecules pushing in all directions and sometimes, there are more on one side than the other, so it fidgets a little. But you will never see a pollen particle jump from one side of the glass to the other, which is basically what happened on Black Monday.

So what really happened twenty years ago? I think of it sort of as a compression of time, kind of like what would happen if the Flash traded stocks. Every minute seems to take as long as a day, so there's no mathematical way to distinguish a drunk stumbling three feet per step for an hour, or the same drunk swerving in a car a couple of hundred feet at a time.

Just as we learned from the Great Depression, there is no reason the same sort of thing can't happen again. But what about politically?

Were the New Deal and Great Society plans of FDR and LBJ the equivalent of a market crash, when suddenly government increased regulation of its citizens by an enormous amount? Perhaps the wars of GWB are similar in that they've certainly increased government power at our expense.

The philosophical lesson is you don't have to participate in the crashes. You don't have to buy or sell, and you don't have to vote left or right. You can withdraw from the market by putting your money in gold, but it's virtually impossible to withdraw from big government. A change in prices of securities around the world, whether it's 5 percent or 20 percent or even 50 percent, is not the end of the world. But an increase of government by the same percentage is quite likely to do harm. At the end of the day, the important things in life aren't securities prices or federal budget line items, they're family and friends and life and love.

So happy birthday, Allan.

Originally published on October 19, 2007

THE THIRD JANUARY EFFECT

You do two things every January: You buy back the stocks you sold in December, and you sign up at a health club. "You," of course, is the hypothetical individual studied by economists, sold to by businesses, and pandered to by politicians (and honored as 2006's person of the Year by Time magazine). But what is the hidden third thing that "you" do every January, as regards your politics?

The financial "January effect" refers to the fact that January has had the best return out of any month for the past 80 years. The typical explanation has been that people sell their stocks in December to create tax losses or to raise cash for the holidays. Then, come January, they buy back those or similar stocks in such quantities that prices soar. The effect is primarily concentrated in stocks with low market capitalization, because those are more strongly affected by the activities of individual investors.

As investors become more aware of the January effect, what happens? If you know prices will soar in January, you'll probably start buying earlier, namely, in December. And that's exactly what's happened. In the past few years, the January effect has been pushed back, and it's really more of a December effect nowadays. Over time, it should dissipate entirely.

This is what economics talk about when they mention the "efficiency" of the market. Once information becomes known, it is incorporated into prices and the effect goes away.

How does that compare to everybody's New Year's resolution to join a gym, eat healthy, and lose weight? January sees the highest enrollments at health clubs, and even a lot of activity. People do actually go the first few days or even weeks. Then, of course, they stop, and when spring rolls around, the gym is empty again.

What's the "January effect" there? It is the belief that this year will be different. It's a powerful belief, and for some people, it works, and they do lose weight and get healthy and exercise often. But for too many of us, we can't seem to keep our word to ourselves.

This is why marketers put very tempting offers out there, like join for free!, or first month's free!, or join now and get free sessions with a trainer. They know all they need to do is get us to commit to a long-term deal and we're stuck. Even if we can cancel, which is often difficult to do, doing so will signal to ourselves that we've given up, we've failed. Continuing to pay the monthly fee may make us feel like we'll go next month—we've just been real busy.

And what of the political "January effect"? What is as predictable, in the political arena, as the stock-market effect and the health club effect?

What's predictable is the ways in which we continue to believe the biggest myth of all: that there are only Democrats on the left and Republicans on the right, and as people of the center, we have to sway with the breeze until we choose one of those directions—or they choose us. In fact, both major parties believe in large government, because they are parties of the government. The size of the pie they slice up is exactly equal to the amount of your money they can wrest control of. Both parties want high taxes and lots of regulations, so that even when they can't buy what they want with money, they can still influence decisions with their regulatory power.

The worst "January effect" of all is that we go to work and start earning, but not keeping, our money. Until around mid-

May, we work for the government. Tax freedom day is defined as that day of the year after which every penny we earn goes into our pockets, and not to federal, state, and local tax collectors. In Connecticut, tax-freedom day comes later than it does in any other state; we work longer each year for the government than any state in the country.

Yet we don't even notice it. It's the hidden "January effect," and the one that adds the most pounds to our waistlines and takes the most money out of our bank accounts.

The solution is the same as for the other effects: Take notice. Once we noticed prices went up in January, we started buying earlier, and the effect disappeared. With health clubs, once we notice that we don't go, we stop signing those long-term contracts. With politics, all we have to do is laugh when the left complains about the right or the right about the left. When we vote for pro-freedom and smaller-government parties like the Libertarians, of which I am a member, the political "January effect" will disappear as well.

Maybe next year, we'll keep all our money without buying too many stocks, or joining too many gyms, or paying too much in taxes. Maybe.

Originally published on January 11, 2007

DID RON PAUL BREAK FOX NEWS?

Two days before the New Hampshire primary, Fox News staged a forum for the Republican presidential candidates and invited everyone who was at the ABC debate the day before, except for Ron Paul. They introduced the forum by saying that the GOP nominee would be one of the five candidates who were there, a statement clearly meant to suggest that Ron Paul doesn't have a chance to win.

That may have been the straw that broke the camel's back, if the camel was an American populace growing increasingly impatient and frustrated with Faux News propaganda.

Fox News wanted to have a forum where it talked with the five GOP candidates who basically agree with their way of thinking: who like the war in Iraq, who like the surge, who want to increase troops in the region, and who have no problem with an eventual war against Iran. What they didn't count on was the depth of support for Ron Paul.

It is hard to measure Paul's support. He is the most-searched-for candidate on the internet, by far, outpacing every Democrat and Republican. He probably raised the most money last quarter (probably, because he reports his donations live while others wait for the FEC deadline at the end of the month). In a graphic map of Meetup groups, other candidates have patches of red dots, while Paul's map is a solid red across the entire country. He has won almost every post-debate poll. Independent Paul supporters have helped him raise $10 million over two days, setting and breaking his own record. There is a blimp flying around the country that asks "Who is Ron Paul?" on one side and suggests you "Google Ron Paul" on the other.

Yet Paul came in fifth in both Iowa and New Hampshire. True, he beat Rudy Giuliani in the first, and nearly tied him in the second, despite the fact that Giuliani apparently spent more time campaigning in both states. But still, the other measures of Paul's support would suggest he should be winning these primaries, possibly by a landslide.

So is the mystery, why does Paul not do better in primaries? Or is the mystery, why does his support seem larger than it is?

It's almost an impossible question to answer. Almost because we now have, thanks to Fox News, proof in the stock market that the support is genuine, and the primary results so far are the aberrations.

The news that Fox News would be excluding Ron Paul from its N.H. debate came on Dec. 27. From that day on, the stock price of News Corp., its parent company, fell every day, losing a cumulative 10 percent, or about $6 billion, over the next seven days.

To be sure, other media companies fell as well. Time Warner and Viacom each fell about 6 percent over that period. The Paul supporters who spread the message of selling News Corp. stock, boycotting Fox News advertisers, and otherwise imposing their economic will cost the media giant billions.

The bleeding stopped Jan. 8, when Fox News relented to the economic pressure and invited Paul to the South Carolina debates. The stock price gained nearly 4 percent in just two days, right back in line with the other media companies.

Those debates were held last week. They were very similar to all the earlier debates, to which Paul had been invited. Other candidates get asked about policy issues while Paul gets asked about his electability. Other candidates snipe at each other and in particular Paul, while Paul ignores them and talks solely about the issues, the only candidate to answer every question that is asked.

But there was one major difference: Whereas in past debates, Paul received a vanishingly small portion of air time, in this one he received approximately equal time. I counted the number of words each candidate uttered. Paul surpassed the word output of John McCain, Mitt Romney, Fred Thompson, and Rudy Giuliani. Only Mike Huckabee said more words.

Maybe it's because Paul talks faster than the others, or because he needed to respond to accusations against him by the other candidates. Or maybe Fox News has realized that the people buttering its proverbial bread are conservatives like Paul and they are trying to recapture that key demographic.

That was, in essence, the only difference in this debate. Everyone else still wants to keep our troops overseas. Everyone else is itching to go to war in Iran at the slightest provocation. Everyone else thinks it is up to the government and the Federal Reserve to stimulate the economy. Only Paul wants to bring our troops home, abolish the IRS, abolish the Federal Reserve, and slash our debt, spending and warring.

On the poll run by Fox News, where viewers can only vote once per cell phone number, the winner of the debate was, as always, Ron Paul.

Originally published on January 17, 2008

RADICAL PURITANS, HESSIANS, AND CHRISTMAS TREES

Should it be illegal to celebrate Christmas? It was when the Puritans ran New England.

The Puritans emigrated to the New World not because they were more tolerant and wanted fewer restrictions, but because they were less tolerant and wanted more laws. Of the ones who arrived in Boston, the extremists among them found the Massachusetts Bay Colony still too lax. For example, since the Bible never mentioned trial by jury, they didn't want it either. These extremists moved first to Hartford, then to New Haven, and finally settled down our own town of Fairfield.

These early-American religious fanatics were responsible for the country's first Blue Laws, passed right here in Connecticut. Those laws criminalized the observance of Christmas, card-playing, dancing, mince-meat pies, and, of course, fornication, which was punishable by enforced marriage. Adultery was punishable by death. Also outlawed were a variety of activities on the Sabbath, including running, walking in your own garden, traveling, making the bed and shaving. Mothers couldn't kiss their own children on the Sabbath (and you thought it was hard enough not being able to buy a beer in Bridgeport on Sunday!).

Pretty strict, those Puritans. Arguably far stricter than the Islamic   fundamentalists we're fighting today. Consider the following laws, all part of the original Blue Laws (they refer to the Colony of Connecticut as "the Dominion"):

1. Conspiracy against this Dominion shall be punished with death.

2. Whoever says there is power and jurisdiction above and over this Dominion, shall suffer death and loss of property.

3. Whoever attempts to change or overturn this Dominion, shall suffer death.

4. If any person turns Quaker, he shall be banished, and not suffered to return but upon pain of death.

Many later immigrants to America, seeking religious freedom, found the Puritans to be far more tyrannical than what they'd fled from. They spread out over the New World and founded other, more tolerant, colonies.

The Puritans gradually lost power and influence. It could be argued that the Salem witch trials were their last hurrah, as they conjured an enemy out of nothing in order to enhance the Puritan's power.

Sound familiar? It should.

In recent years, Washington has passed law after law taking away our hard-fought liberties, from the Patriot Act to the unconstitutional invasion of Iraq, to the Military Commissions Act, to all the hundreds and thousands of little "mince-meat pie" types of regulations we live under.

And it's not just one party trying to hold on to power while the other champions freedom. Both ruling parties endorse these invasions on our liberties, and do so with open arms.

The two-party system is no different from the Puritans. Under the Puritans, no one was allowed to vote unless they belonged to one of the few approved churches of the Dominion. Today we call those religions Democrat and Republican.

Libertarians like myself are the modern-day heretics arguing for more freedom. The Puritans forbade heretics from holding elected office. Our two-party system makes it virtually impossible for a third-party candidate to get elected, even if he is the best choice. The Puritans did not allow heretics to even receive food or lodging from anyone. As the two major parties clamor for more and more campaign-finance regulations, third-party candidates often find themselves shut out of the fund-raising system.

When the New World was young and Puritanical government small and local, there were plenty of nearby places to go to find freedom. But what do you do, where do you go, when the federal government is taking away your liberties?

We should take a cue from the actions of Samuel Denslow, a farmer from Windsor Locks during the Revolutionary War era. He took custody of a prisoner of war named Henrick Roddmore, one of many Germany mercenaries (Hessians) hired by the British during the war. The Christmas tree started as a German tradition and Roddmore apparently convinced Denslow to try it out. For 14 years, Roddmore would erect a tree inside Denslow's Connecticut home.

It was the first Christmas tree in America.

That's our secret weapon and the source of our internal political conflict: The same state that saw some of the most extreme Puritanical tyranny also saw one of the first steps toward religious freedom. The longing to do right has always defined Connecticut. We want people to be moral here; we also yearn for freedom.

Originally published on December 20, 2006

Good news, frolicking girls and slackjawed boys! You no longer need to fly south for the winter to be caught on tape performing arguably illicit activities. In a few weeks, you can simply set foot in the city of Stamford and wave a hearty hello to the new surveillance cameras. Big Brother has come to Stamford, and he's got lots of DVDs to burn.

It's no big deal for those of us who don't want government looking over every shoulder: Just steer clear of any "public streets, public rights of way, property owned by any governmental agency or body politic... or locations identified as critical assets by the State of Connecticut." In other words, stay indoors with the shades down.

When Stamford first authorized video cameras to help monitor traffic patterns, there was, understandably, a hue and a cry that such cameras aren't used for any other purpose. Indeed, Stamford law prohibits the use of such cameras for warrantless surveillance.

But that law is likely to change. Those same video cameras, and other "technological devices," can and will be used for law enforcement and for homeland security. They'll be placed in high-crime areas, near public housing projects, and around schools and day-care centers. They'll still pretend to use them for traffic monitoring—but soon enough, what our elected officials will be monitoring is the drug traffic.

This issue gives pause even to me, an avowed Libertarian. On the one hand, I would obviously prefer the government do less surveillance on innocent civilians. On the other, we do have police. In principle, we could have as many police as we have video cameras, each just standing around, enforcing the law and providing homeland security. I support local governments having a police force to combat crime and catch criminals. So why would video cameras, especially if they are cheaper and can reduce taxes, not be a good idea?

First, there is a limit to how large a police force needs to be before it stops being an agent for justice and becomes a tool of oppression. A few cops here and there can enhance safety, deter crime, and promote justice by being able to quickly catch lawbreakers. But how would you feel if we had a cop on every street corner, in every cafe? You'd start to feel occupied, not liberated.

But more cops would be better than more video cameras. Why? Because video cameras can't stop bad guys. Video cameras can't hear a woman's scream from a block away, a block that happens not to be covered on video, and go running to help. Video cameras can't walk you to your car if you feel unsafe.

There are, of course, all the standard arguments against government using video cameras for surveillance, namely, abuse of power. Operators of the cameras can tend to focus on "suspicious" looking people, where suspicion is defined by skin color. Operators have also been known to use video cameras to peep.

The biggest reason video cameras are bad? They put the chill on free speech and freedom of assembly. If you're going out for dinner and a walk, would you go to a place where you and your antics will be caught on film, available to anyone filing the appropriate Freedom of Information Act request? Or would you like to go somewhere where you wouldn't have to worry about the possible embarrassment, or worse, of being caught on film?

Given that they present such an obvious restriction on liberty, why would a government ever agree to these ubiquitous video cameras? Two words: homeland security.

But it's not yet too late to do something about this.

We have a couple of weeks to enjoy Stamford without feeling like we're in a Vegas casino with black domes everywhere. In that week, we can stop by and grab a sandwich at the local deli in freedom for one last time, and maybe petition the city to back off before its motto is changed to The City That Lurks.

Your chance to do that is on Jan. 31, at 7 p.m., in the Democratic caucus room at 888 Washington Blvd. There's a public hearing that night before the legislation moves to a final vote before the City Council on Feb. 5.

Originally published on January 18, 2007

Groundhogs, Romans, Indians, and Robocalls

Every February 2nd, a groundhog pops out of the ground. If he sees his shadow, we get six more weeks of winter. That's the folklore. But all is not as it seems.

To begin with, that's not even the complete lore. What happens if he doesn't see his shadow? Originally it meant we'd have only 42 more days of winter. But as anybody familiar with Douglas Adams knows, six times seven is 42, the answer to life, the universe, and everything. Six weeks is exactly 42 days. What gives?

The groundhog tradition has its root in the fifth century when Rome fell to Attila the Hun. Attila's people believed that certain animals had special powers on days halfway between the winter solstice and the spring equinox. It was also believed that hibernating animals like bears and groundhogs who woke up too early would go back to sleep for six more weeks. The falling of Rome is today one of the biggest events in the history of the world. Imagine what it must have felt like back then to see your entire empire collapse nearly overnight.

What would you do if you were invaded by a foreign people with strange beliefs? If you could, you'd ridicule them, but secretly and quietly, in a way they don't notice, much like Soviet authors used metaphor and analogy to sneak digs at the Communists past the censors. The freedoms of speech and expression are among any military government's first casualties. Back then, the Romans were still on the Julian calendar, and the spring equinox fell on March 16, exactly six weeks after February 2. The Romans came to call it Hedgehog Day. All is not as it seems. It was a joke. Humor is the last defense of a free man.

But that's not all. The groundhog, also known as the woodchuck, is not a hog, and has nothing to do with wood. It comes from the Narragansett word wuchak.

The Narragansett are a once-flourishing Native American tribe that controlled parts of Connecticut, Massachusetts, and Rhode Island for thousands of years, probably dating back to the same fifth century when Attila was conquering Rome. In addition to the woodchuck, we use many other words borrowed from the Narragansetts, including squash, succotash, papoose, powwow, and quahog, the clam and Rhode Island city made famous by Family Guy.

What happened to the Narragansett tribe? Why are there now less than 3,000 remaining? Thanks go to King Philip's war. But remember: all is not as it seems. King Philip was neither a king nor named Philip. He was Metacomet, the leader of the allied Native Americans from southern New England who fought the English in 1675. Part of the cause for the war was the demand by the Puritans that the Indians turn over all their firearms. Self-defense, along with free speech, is always a top casualty of iron-fist rulers. King Philip's war was probably the bloodiest ever waged in North America. One in ten people of both sides were wounded or killed. For comparison, the Bubonic plague, the worst killer of humans ever, killed one in three people. And to bring it all full circle, the Bubonic plague was likely carried not by rats as commonly assumed, but by marmots like our friend the groundhog.

What's amazing is that our founding fathers recognized these important freedoms and made sure, as best they could, that our government would not infringe on them. Yet here we are, with our freedom to bear arms restricted in many ways, and our freedom to speak being squeezed out bit by bit.

The latest assault on our freedom of speech comes on both a federal level, thanks in large part to our Representative in Congress, Republican Christopher Shays, and on a state level right here in Connecticut, as various laws have now been proposed to put an end to robocalls, those annoying automated political phone calls.

When I ran against Shays, and Democrat Diane Farrell, this past election, I was both a user of robocalls, and a victim of their abuse. I used an automated program to call a small sample of registered voters to poll them on who they would vote for. I had to do it to show the few debate organizers who wanted to exclude me from their events that I had solid support, but it ended up not making a difference. They only wanted the two ruling parties represented at their debates, which turned out to be far less interesting than the seven debates in which I did participate. And I heard that other robocalls were placed by somebody, we still don't know by who, to tell people not to listen to what I say, after I ran several ads showing there was essentially no difference between my opponents, or Democrats and Republicans in general, when it came to questions of taxes or the war in Iraq. Those ads are still available on my campaign website.

Reportedly the robocall about me said it came from the Diane Farrell campaign but she told me personally her campaign hadn't authorized any robocalls at all, let alone that one, and I believe her. We also received word from the Shays campaign that they hadn't done any robocalls either, and I believe them too.

Theft and deceit and fraud are already illegal and I'm sure if I wanted to sue somebody, we could dig up who was responsible. The two proposed laws that Shays is co-sponsoring on a federal level and that are also under discussion for our state are similar to each other. They seek to prohibit "politically oriented recorded messages made to telephone numbers on the Do-Not-Call registry."

Seems reasonable, right? The calls are annoying and if we can make them illegal when the recipient has already optionally registered with the government's do-not-call list, it's a great thing, right? But remember: all is not as it seems.

These pieces of legislation add to the already existing campaign regulations that limit donations, force campaigns to file personal information of their supporters, and insist on stupid disclaimers like "I approve this message." Bit by bit, the Democrats and Republicans are making it so that only approved candidates can run for office. It is already nearly impossible to run unless you belong to one of their parties, even though more people are registered Independent.

Isn't voting the bad guys out our last defense against corruption? We should make it easier, not harder, for people to speak to each other and contact each other. Anybody can get caller ID and choose not to pickup anonymous calls. There shouldn't be a government-run do-not-call registry at all. Would you pay your phone company to guarantee you don't receive any telemarketers or robocalls, ever? Obviously such a service is possible. If you wouldn't pay but want the benefit, why should someone else pay for you through their taxes?

The government's role should be to defend and maximize our freedoms, not sell them for political gain. We should eliminate the obsolete telephone taxes to slash our monthly bills, get rid of NSA restrictions on satellites so we can have better cell coverage, remove any law protecting telephone monopolies so we have more choice, and keep the Internet free so we have better service by preventing regulations such as the Orwellianly named "net neutrality" laws.

The government wants to twist our tongues so we can't speak in a way that offends them. The most famous tongue-twister of all is, of course, about our February friend. How much wood would a woodchuck chuck if a woodchuck could chuck wood? How many freedoms would a politician limit if a politician could limit freedoms?

The point is that woodchucks don't chuck wood and politicians shouldn't be able to limit our freedoms.

But who do we turn to when the ones who are supposed to defend our freedoms against all enemies, foreign and domestic, are the very ones who are taking them away?

This Groundhog day, it's time for us to awake from our political hibernation and open our eyes to the shadows that Washington has been casting over us for far too long. It's time to end our two-party winter.

And if you wake up and don't see anything different, just remember: all is not as it seems.

Originally published on February 2, 2007

That headline translates roughly to *So swallows the glory of the world* or *Taste is fleeting*.

Do you think lawmakers in Hartford should decide what you can eat when you go out in Greenwich or Stamford or Norwalk? Do you think they should keep unhealthy options away from you?

They've taken one step closer to banning trans fats from being used in any restaurant in the state, not because the production of trans fats uses child labor, not to reduce our dependence on foreign trans fats, and not even because trans fats deplete the ozone. None of those tired excuses for interfering in your life were even trotted out.

This was pure paternalism. They think it's bad for you. Therefore, you shouldn't have the option to decide otherwise.

Can't a guy even eat a nice, greasy basket of fries anymore without the nanny state slapping his hand?

Eating trans fat does not cause more crime or put pushers on school grounds ("Hey, buddy, want some trans fat?" is not a commonly heard schoolyard expression).

The worst possible thing trans fat will do is kill you, and you alone—if you eat way too much of it. But it's your life. Who gets to make decisions about your life and the amount of risk you can take?

Can you go skydiving? Rock climbing? Can you attempt to hike Mount Everest, or should we file papers for permission from Connecticut's Senate Deputy Minority Leader John McKinney (R-Fairfield), one of the co-sponsors of the trans fat legislation?

Can you take stressful or dangerous jobs? Can you drive a car? Can you eat raw fish on rice? Can you enlist and ship out to Iraq?

No one ever forced you to eat trans fats. You can go to another restaurant, or start your own, or eat at home, or order different food.

You may not even want the choice of eating trans fat, since you, a healthy person, would never choose it anyway. Perhaps you are okay with this legislation, even though it was underhandedly tacked on as an amendment to a bill to repair a swimming pool.

If you are okay with them making those kinds of decisions for you, then logically you should be okay with them telling you what kind of healthy career opportunities are available to you, what kind of healthy spouses you can marry, what kind of friends you can have, and what kind of person you can vote for, especially if the options they take away from you are ones you weren't really considering anyway.

The real issue isn't even about the trans fat. It's about who runs your life when not a single other person is even remotely involved. As an aside, if you think the government should make this decision for you because otherwise you would be eating up public funds with health-care costs, then that same logic applies to the government deciding your friends, job, dates, hobbies, etc., because otherwise you might be depressed or hospitalized and take up public funds again.

The problem is the size of the government. You can bathe in trans fat in your own home if you want to, because that's out of the government jurisdiction. If they could, they'd regulate that too, but they can't, so they stick to regulating restaurants, because for some reason we've allowed them that leeway without any limits on what they can do with that power.

To paraphrase a famous poem by Martin Niemöller:

First they took the alcohol, and I didn't speak up, because I wasn't an alcoholic.

Then they took the marijuana, and I didn't speak up, because I wasn't a pothead.

Then they took the tobacco, and I didn't speak up, because I didn't smoke.

Then they took the trans fats, and I didn't speak up, because I didn't eat it anyway.

Then they took the chocolates, and I didn't speak up, because I didn't have a sweet tooth.

Then they took my TV and internet, and by that time, there was no one to speak up for me.

They were all at the gym working out.

And I hate exercise.

If you let the government take away this choice from you by force, you are authorizing them to do it about other choices as well, and you won't be able to argue later that it's none of their concern. And the next choice they take away might be something you used to like.

Originally published on May 23, 2007

We should not have speed limits on our largest highways, at least not in the left-most lane, and here's why.

Speed limits have virtually nothing to do with safety. People who speed are not necessarily unsafe, and unsafe drivers don't necessarily speed. In fact, it is already illegal to drive dangerously, regardless of what the posted speed limit is. If a cop thinks you are driving too fast, too slow, or too erratically for the conditions of the road at the time, then you can be charged with reckless driving.

And it does make sense to have troopers look out for reckless drivers because they pose a danger. But that doesn't mean it's right to indiscriminately stop those who go "too fast."

On highways, speed and safety are unrelated. Once you're going beyond 40 miles per hour, any collision is going to be painful. The Connecticut Department of Transportation agrees: It prominently states on its website that lowering speed limits does not reduce accident frequency.

"Accidents are most often the result of driver inattention and driver error," according to the department. It also admits that speed limits set too low will create too much variability in driving speeds and thus lead to more accidents.

So safety is not the primary concern for speed limits on highways. The primary benefits of speed limits are the revenues collected from speeders, which explains why the speed limits tend to be too low: that way, they can catch more speeders.

Speed limits shouldn't be a hidden tax.

Beyond the costs of speeding tickets, lost time in court, and higher insurance premiums, there is the much bigger cost of wasted time on the road.

Consider a commuter who travels 60 minutes each way to work, with ten of those minutes on local roads. He averages the speed limit of 65 miles per hour for the other 50 minutes. If he were to travel at 90 miles per hour—if he could drive that fast, assuming the roads weren't too congested—then he would cut his total commute down by almost 15 minutes each way. That's a half hour saved per day. In a year, that's 126 hours, or more than three full working weeks. It's like having an extra three weeks of vacation spread out over the course of the year.

Now multiply that by the more than 100,000 people who drive on Connecticut's I-95 each day, and assume they each earn $20 an hour on average, which is probably low since commuters tend to be higher earners. So continuing to force them all to drive at 65 miles per hour has an opportunity cost of more than $250 million per year. Every four years we waste an extra billion dollars by driving too slowly.

Plus there are civil liberty issues. One man in Texas, pulled over for going 70 in a 65 zone, got Tasered for not showing his license and registration quickly enough. A Utah man, pulled over for speeding, got Tasered in front of his pregnant wife and baby. Every excuse we give to the government to arrest us results in more abuses. Again, this is not to say police should not pull over reckless drivers—they should, regardless of the speed they are driving—but it is important to recognize that the more people they can pull over, the more often civil liberties will be abused. And hasn't the government abused us enough?

We should stop giving them excuses.

Originally published on December 20, 2007

Is it merely a coincidence that the last three catastrophic bridge disasters resulting from structural failures were all interstate highways?

The collapse of the I-35W Mississippi River bridge in Minneapolis last week that killed at least four and injured dozens more gruesomely recalls the last two structural bridge tragedies, both of which happened in our neck of the woods.

Twenty years ago, the Schoharie Creek I-90 thruway bridge collapsed because of poor maintenance, killing ten and wounding untold others. Four years before that, a 100-foot section of the northbound lanes of the Mianus River bridge between exits 4 and 5 on I-95 in Greenwich collapsed due to poor inspection, killing three and wounding three others as two trucks and two cars plummeted 70 feet into the void.

The common thread is that all three were bridges serving interstate highways: I-35W in Minneapolis, I-90 in New York, and I-95 right here in Fairfield County.

Three, of course, is not a statistically significant sample in virtually any context. Additionally, our Interstate Highway System has a total length of nearly 50,000 miles, or about 30 percent of the 160,000 miles of America's largest roads, so even by random chance one in three catastrophes would likely be of federally-funded interstate highways.

But the wide reach of the government, both federal and state, shouldn't act as an excuse for failure. Even if every inch of road in America was federally funded, any bridge collapse is one too many. Of the 27 global catastrophic bridge collapses listed by Wikipedia since 1940, nine were in America. Germany was in second place with five.

Does it matter that the highways are federally funded? After all, it is the responsibility of the state to use those funds to build and maintain the roads and bridges (the only exception is the federally managed Woodrow Wilson Bridge in Washington, D.C.). Indeed, the consensus report after the Mianus River disaster of 1983 was that Connecticut was woefully deficient in its bridge inspection and maintenance. At the time, we employed 12 engineers who worked in pairs to inspect 3,425 bridges.

The answer is yes, it does matter, for three reasons.

Number one, it further decouples the costs from the benefits in decisions of where, when, and how to build roads. The best decision is made when the decision maker faces both the costs and the benefits. When you decide to repave your driveway, you will make the optimal decision for you, because you face virtually all of the costs and benefits yourself. When you live on a private road, you and your neighbors share some of the costs and some of the benefits in non-identical ways, i.e., some use less of the road than others, so it is likely to be a less optimal decision than if one person owned the whole thing, but the costs and benefits are still very localized. When a town hikes taxes to repair roads, they are essentially redistributing money from those that live far from the repairs to landowners near the repairs. You can start to imagine the conflicts of interest as small groups lobby for construction and maintenance where it is best for them. When it moves to the state level, it gets even worse. When it becomes federally funded, we end up with bridges to nowhere in Alaska and other pork roads as politicians funnel money to their states at our expense.

Number two, it increases our taxes and creates perverse incentives to look as pathetic as possible to beg for more of our own money back. We pay more in federal taxes than we receive in federal money back, and even the money we do get back, whether it's for highways or schools, is not spent the way we would have spent it if we had just kept our money.

Number three, federal money comes with dirty strings attached. You can't spend the cash as you would like, simply hiring the most efficient or reliable workers. No, you must cater to Washington's political demands, even when they are racist, unfair, and counterproductive, such as the Davis-Bacon act. Passed in 1931 with obvious discriminatory intent to keep cheaper migrant black workers from being employed by states using federal money, it requires workers be paid "prevailing wages," typically defined by the local unions, which at the time were groups of expensive white workers. The law is still on the books and it is still enforced: You are not allowed to find good deals as a matter of law. In addition, the federal government has often threatened to withhold funds unless states pass other laws. Some examples: speed limits, drinking ages, disclosing the identities of sex offenders, lowering the allowable level of intoxication, and requiring carpool lanes. Those should all be state decisions but the federal government teases us with our own money until we live how they say we should.

Can bridges and roads be built without federal assistance? Until 1956, they all were. That year, President Eisenhower, jealous of the German Autobahn, pushed through the Federal-Aid Highway Act, claiming we could have a national highway system built for $25 billion in 12 years. The final tally was $114 billion over 35 years.

Would roads and bridges built with our own money and for our own needs be safer? Unfortunately, they would almost have to be.

Originally published on August 8, 2007

The only justification for the ever-expanding powers of the federal government, both in overseas military activities and in domestic surveillance of its own citizens, is in preventing acts of terror. Push any supporter of the war in Iraq and eventually they will say something like "Better to fight them over there than over here." Pester any supporter of the Patriot Act and they will argue that a small, hypothetical invasion of privacy is a small price to pay to foil terrorist plots.

Both camps will point to a range of successes, actual terrorist attempts thwarted by information collected in an unscrupulous manner, whether by torture or Taser, by waterboarding or wiretapping. Indeed both camps are two sides of the same devilish coin, on which is embossed their mutual motto: The ends justify the means.

The ends are to prevent another 9/11. There are basically no limitations on the means, except perhaps on the rate of growth. Like a virus, the means tend to grow slowly, waiting until we are accustomed to one before imposing another. National ID cards, mandatory tracking databases, roving wiretaps, and perhaps even reinstating the draft are all more than just possibilities: They have all been introduced and sometimes passed by Congress.

Why stop there? Let's imagine for a moment that the government has the technology to unobtrusively read our minds. Should we let them do it?

One answer would be to allow it as any search is allowed: with a proper warrant duly issued by an independent judge on the basis of reasonable suspicion of criminal activity. In this case, the technology would have to stand up to rigorous standards. It would be the state's burden to prove that it is effective, accurate, and unlikely to result in false positives (incorrectly classifying innocents as criminals). After all, who among us hasn't had harmless assassination fantasies that end with a glorious return to our libertarian roots? (Dear Secret Service: not me. Assassination is un-libertarian. I fantasize about a non-violent return to freedom. Good times!)

The other answer, the answer of the devilish coin, is to allow mind-reading so long as the data is used only to prevent future terrorist plots and is well-protected. We wouldn't want all that information to fall into the wrong hands. In this case, the technology can even be ineffective, faulty, and biased, so long as it helps stop a crime or two.

If you support the war in Iraq or other preventive wars, or national ID cards, warrantless wiretapping, or any of the other intrusions on our privacies, then you hold in your pocket the devilish coin and its motto is your mantra. To be consistent, you must also endorse a universal application of the government's mind-reading device.

This isn't science fiction. The British Guardian reported last week that scientists have developed a method using MRI scans that can accurately predict the images people are thinking of. In a test where random guessing would have resulted in less than one correct prediction out of a hundred, their method correctly predicted ninety.

Of course, requiring all Americans to lie in MRI machines for hours at a time is still a few years off. (First we need to be issued national ID cards with magnetic strips to facilitate processing.) But there is actually a better and simpler technology already available. Why not let the government listen to your phone calls, read your emails, and track your web traffic?

It wouldn't even be very invasive. No human agents even need to be involved unless reasonable red flags appear, like if the word assassination appears anywhere near Patriot Act or Iraq or libertarian. (Are you reading the online version of this article? Wait for a knock on your door.)

If you don't like this scenario, ask yourself where you would draw the line. Words like reasonable are inappropriate here, because the government, and the people, could decide that all of this is reasonable, but that still wouldn't make it justifiable.

There is no fuzzy gray line here. The government should not initiate force against innocent people. Period. (Neither should anyone else—that's all of libertarianism in a nutshell.)

The devilish coin should be tossed—into the wastebasket.

Originally published on March 13, 2008

THE THREE AMIGOS: CLINTON, OBAMA, AND MCCAIN

The next president will likely either be Barack Obama, Hillary Clinton or John McCain. Isn't it nice to finally have a choice? A middle-aged black man, an older white woman, and an even older white man. Liberals and conservatives. Left and right. Finally, we have some genuine differences in policy to debate. Right?

Of course not.

First, ignore skin color, gender, and age. They mean nothing. Second, discount the rhetoric. We all know the value of a politician's word. Instead, look to their actions. What we have here is a race among three senators. So let's compare their voting record.

I got the voting records of each of the three amigos from Project Vote Smart (vote-smart.org), which maintains a collection of key votes going back to 1995. McCain has cast 774 votes since 1995, Clinton 507 since 2001, and Obama 392 since 2005.

Let's try to find out how often they voted the same way.

I'll describe the methods and the results but in the meantime, let your subconscious ponder this question: what numbers should you expect? If we are really being offered a choice, then McCain should disagree nearly 100 percent of the time with Obama and Clinton. But what about the two Democrats? Surely they have some common ground. Maybe they disagree half the time. Think of a person with whom you disagree politically. What percent of the time would you say you disagree? Half the time? Nearly all the time?

Here's how I calculated everything. Each vote is a Yay, a Nay, or a No-Vote. An important question is: what should a No-Vote count as? Suppose McCain abstained from a vote that both Obama and Clinton favored. Does that mean McCain opposed it or tacitly favored it?

Consider how you vote in an election. If you vote for Ron Paul but John McCain wins, then you clearly voted against McCain, and you have the moral right to object to McCain's leadership. But if you sat at home and didn't vote for anybody, then, like most Americans, you basically don't care, and you are tacitly approving whoever emerges as victor.

Using that logic, I count a non-vote as a tacit agreement. If a senator thought a particular bill was unconstitutional, unholy, or just plain un-American, he or she could and should have voted against it. That's their job—it's basically their only duty. If they don't vote against it, they are essentially for it. Similarly, if a senator thought a particular bill was good, but failed to vote for it, then they are essentially against it. For example, a bill that would do good things but happens to be unconstitutional should be actively voted against, each and every time. To abstain from voting in such an instance is a dereliction of duty.

To the results. Let's start with McCain-Obama. So what does your subconscious think the portion of agreement should be between these two? Maybe they should agree 2 percent of the time? 3? 5?

McCain and Obama had 248 overlapping votes, that is, bills on which each voted. Out of those 248, they agreed, either tacitly or directly, a whopping 121 times. That's just under fifty percent.

McCain and Clinton were similar, agreeing 202 times out 361, for a little more than fifty percent.

And Obama vs. Clinton? The two Democrats agreed on 240 out of 248 bills. That's a 97 percent agreement.

So where is our variety? Where is our real debate? The two Democrats are virtually identical, and the Republican agrees with them more than he disagrees.

The Three Amigos was a 1986 comedy in which Steve Martin, Chevy Chase, and Martin Short play three actors asked to reprise their roles as heroes and defenders, only they don't realize until it is too late that they are fighting a real enemy. Their catchphrase was:

Amigo 1: Wherever there is injustice, you will find us. Amigo 2: Wherever there is suffering, we'll be there. Amigo 3: Wherever liberty is threatened, you will find... All together: The Three Amigos!

The funny thing about the catchphrase is it makes it sound as if the three amigos are responsible for the injustice, suffering, and threatened liberties. Of course, in real life, it's not so funny anymore.

Especially now that we have no real choice left.

Originally published on February 14, 2008

BORDERLINE INSANITY: WHAT ABOUT TURKMENISTAN?

Iran has 3,300 miles of land bordering seven countries. By comparison, our southern border (the one we can't seem to control) extends 2,000 miles and only has Mexico on the other side. And it seems that we are doing everything we can to surround Iran.

We've invaded Iraq and installed about 150,000 troops. Iran's border with Iraq is its longest with a single country, about 1,000 miles. 1,200 miles of its eastern border is split between Afghanistan, where we have another 25,000 troops, and Pakistan, allegedly our strongest ally in the region and the beneficiary of billions of foreign-aid dollars. Of course, Iran also has a 1,500-mile coastline on the Persian Gulf—and guess whose warships now float menacingly along those waters.

How would we feel if China were to invade Mexico and Canada, establish permanent bases in each, and line up submarines a few miles past the Statue of Liberty? They would issue no threats to us. They would just sit there and wait. That's where we are today with Iran—baiting them, waiting for them to give us an excuse.

Just as we waited in 1915 when the *Lusitania* sank, leading us into WWI. Just as we waited in 1964 when Vietnam allegedly attacked two American destroyers in the Gulf of Tonkin, leading us into the Vietnam War. Both events were contrived or at least facilitated to bolster public support for wars.

A few weeks ago, an exaggerated encounter with some Iranian speedboats was almost used as an excuse to attack a country whose size and population is larger than the total of Texas, California, and all of New England.

The real question is: How does Turkmenistan fit in? Yes, Turkmenistan. The former part of the Soviet Union is essentially a dictatorship that shares a critical 600-mile border on Iran's northern end. And of course you haven't heard anything about it—yet.

American troops have Iran and its president, Mahmoud Ahmadinejad, surrounded on the west, the east, and the south. But Turkmenistan provides the north. Turkey does share a 300-mile border on Iran's northwest, but Turkey is far more easily defensible.

The combination of Turkey, Turkmenistan, Afghanistan, Pakistan, and Iraq comprises about 90 percent of the land bordering Iran.

Turkmenistan has, or at least had, strong trading relationships with Iran and Afghanistan. Of course, that was before they saw the writing on the wall that we are all still too afraid to see—that Iran is in danger.

Curiously, two years after we invaded Iraq, Turkmenistan partially withdrew from the Commonwealth of Independent States, the federation of former Soviet republics. Its leaders claim it wanted to follow a policy of permanent neutrality. Can they see what we dare not admit: that a war against Iran is a war against Russia? That it begets a global war?

The Turkmens are still intricately tied in with Russia as they sell about two-thirds of their gas through Gazprom. But would they become an American ally? What would it cost? And have we already started negotiating with them?

Perhaps we have. Turkmenistan is pondering building expensive pipelines underneath the Caspian Sea to have a better gateway to Europe and the rest of the West, bypassing Gazprom. And for a country that hasn't had its leader visit the United States in ten years, isn't it a little surprising the first such visit came just three months ago?

Is Turkmenistan playing Russia and America off of each other to get the highest bid for its important border with Iran?

Start keeping an eye out for Turkmenistan. Once you start hearing it on the news, that will mean we have "won" the bidding. The losers will be our civil liberties, our safety, our earnings, the value of our dollar, and peace.

Originally published on January 31, 2008

Ron Paul is not your typical Republican presidential candidate, and that's unfortunate for the Grand Ol' Party. He's the only one of ten GOP candidates who opposed the war in Iraq and he's the only one who opposed the Patriot Act. Even Hillary Clinton and Barak Obama voted in favor of the Patriot Act, and Clinton voted in favor of the war in 2003. During the first debate between the crowded Republican field of candidates, Paul was asked if he really ought to be running as a Democrat. That's a chilling indictment on the party of the first Ron, Ronald Reagan.

Republicans used to stand for limited government, low taxes, freedom, and liberty. Is Ron Paul the only such Republican left?

Only among the politicians. The people have overwhelmingly endorsed him to the point where political pundits are scratching their heads trying to figure out why Paul has such staggering internet support. After the debates, he is consistently voted the winner, or, at worst, the second-place winner. The look on conservative commentator Sean Hannity's face when he saw his own station's polls had Paul in the lead was priceless. Paul has more subscribers on YouTube, MySpace, and Eventful.com than any other presidential candidate of either party. His YouTube videos have been viewed more than a million times, more than any other candidate other than Obama. For a while, the term "Ron Paul" was the number-one search phrase on the internet. Paris Hilton, by way of contrast, was fifth.

What is it that is so appealing about Paul? I think it is the same thing that people found appealing about Ronald Reagan: a consistent and passionate love of freedom. Both of them never wavered from their principles over a period of decades. Both believed that in most cases, government is the problem, and freedom the solution. Both believed in a strong military for defensive purposes only, not empire building.

Before Paul was a United States congressman, he was a medical doctor who delivered thousands of babies. Not once during his medical career did he accept Medicare payments. Instead, he would lower or waive his fees.

He doesn't participate in the congressional pension program. He has never voted for a congressional pay increase. He returns part of his congressional office budget to the U.S. Treasury each year.

He has never, ever, *ever* voted to increase taxes. And he's been in congress for ten terms.

I am almost jealous of people who are just now hearing about Ron Paul for the first time. It's like seeing someone start to read Harry Potter from the beginning or watch *The Matrix* for the first time. You know they are going to be blown away and their life changed forever.

I can't even remember when I first found out about him. Though we've never met, he's been a constant in my life for as long as I can remember. When I ran for congress last year on the Libertarian ticket to represent Fairfield County, it pleased me enormously to know that had I won, he and I would have been colleagues. He is one of those people that you are glad is out there. At least there's one decent member of congress, you think. At least someone will vote against unconstitutional bills.

Ron Paul does that better than anybody. He once described how he and his staff read the bills. They start on page one and stop as soon as they see something that violates the Constitution. Rarely do they have to read past page two. It is a rare bill indeed that gets read to the end without violating the rights and liberties of Americans. This process has earned him the moniker "Dr. No," though his wife prefers thinking of it as the less-negative-sounding "Dr. Know."

Political pundits can't figure out why Ron Paul has such strong internet support. They think there is some sort of gimmick or hack because there can't possibly be so many people who care about liberty!

Can there?

Yes, there can. Large sites such as Technorati.com have confirmed the online support is genuine and widespread.

So what is going on? Why such strong internet support but weak polling support? He now registers around 3 to 5 percent support in polls, up from 1 percent a few short months ago, and fifth overall behind the leading candidates Rudy Giuliani, Mitt Romney, John McCain, and Fred Thompson. Even on sports gambling sites where people can put up their own money, the free market believes he has about a 2 percent chance of winning.

But here's the kicker: People are just now learning about this underdog for freedom. Ron Paul has very low name recognition but very favorable appeal among people who do know him. As more people find out about him, they overwhelmingly support him. There are not many candidates about whom that can be said.

The only question is if enough people find out about him before the primaries.

One thing that's helped is appearing on *The Daily Show* and *The Colbert Report*, earning large cheers every time. Last week, Stephen Colbert listed various organizations and asked which of them Paul would abolish or withdraw American membership from.

The Department of Education. The Department of Homeland Security. The Department of Energy. The Internal Revenue Service. FEMA. The U.N. NATO. The Interstate Commerce Commission. NAFTA. The WTO. UNICEF.

Could you have imagined any politician, let alone a presidential candidate, speaking so candidly about abolishing so many agencies? It's no wonder that even though he's in his eighth decade of life and second decade of being a congressman, Paul's still a fresh face. "You are an enigma wrapped in a riddle nestled in a sesame seed bun of mystery," Colbert told him last week. "I'm a Constitutionalist," Paul replied. "And you haven't met one in a long time."

Indeed we haven't, but it seems we've been itching to. In Fairfield County, we tend to lean toward the Democratic ticket when it comes to presidential elections, but we've elected a Republican Congressman for the past twenty years. We are vehemently against Iraq yet we are even more vehemently against taxes. We pay far more to the federal government in taxes than we get back through various federal agencies, all of which Ron Paul would abolish. In many ways, his positions on the issues seem to mirror our own. For the first time, we don't have to choose between two candidates, each of whom agrees with us about fifty percent.

Recently I had a chance to ask him some questions. True to his internet persona, we communicated mainly by email and text message as he was on the train to and from taping *Colbert*. If I didn't know better, I'd assume he was 40 years younger. In fact, he'll turn 72 in August, about the same age Reagan was as president.

I learned from my campaign for congress that tough questions are more fun. Sharper questions elicit a better understanding of the person answering them. They also help separate the principled politicians from the wafflers. And they are more fun to read. So, the premise behind each question is to assume Ron Paul is president of the United States.

How and when would you get out of Iraq?

I would start by redirecting our military to appropriate activities—not policing the streets. From there, the process and logistics to transition our troops home would have to be worked out responsibly.

If you had been president in 2000, what military cutbacks would you have implemented in your first few months in office? Assuming 9/11 would have happened anyway, what would your response have been?

I would have started to remove any unnecessary troops stationed abroad and bring them home. In the aftermath when congress was deciding how to respond, I proposed we implement the constitutional option of issuing Letters of Marque and Reprisal to target Osama bin Laden and others responsible, instead of bombing civilian populations while he runs free.

If an Arab country attacks Israel, should America react with military force? Under what conditions?

As a general principle I support a foreign policy of non-intervention. I would respond if the conditions of the attack on Israel threatened U.S. national security. On the other hand, I would not violate Israel's sovereignty by telling her how to handle her own foreign policy.

The average Fairfield County household pays about $60,000 in federal taxes per year, mainly in income and payroll taxes, the highest in the nation. What would you estimate would be our tax bill with you as president?

I have not crunched the numbers on what that estimate would be; however, we could easily reduce government spending by reducing our commitments overseas fighting wars, policing the world and subsidizing the security of other wealthy nations. We could save hundreds of billions of dollars every year, allowing us to cut taxes and balance the budget.

Many if not most hedge funds are based in Fairfield County. Should they be regulated at all? Should mutual funds be regulated? Should the Securities and Exchange Commission continue to exist? If not, who will protect unsophisticated investors from making poor choices?

There is no such thing as an unregulated market. Markets should be regulated by free choice rather than by government. History strongly suggests that the private markets react faster than governmental regulations and therefore are more likely to correct problems when they are smaller and do not threaten systemic risk. Certainly anti-fraud provisions are justified and provide a sound basis for the mutual fund industry. Subjective valuations of "poor choices" should depend on the consumer and their advisers complying with state consumer laws.

You plan to eliminate the Federal Reserve. How would that transition happen? Would you allow competing currencies to the dollar? What would happen when people want to withdraw more money than a bank has on hand and there is no Fed for them to borrow from overnight?

My plan would be to first legalize the use of gold and silver to be used as legal tender for major transactions. Legalizing commodities to compete with dollars will help stabilize the dollar and fight inflation.

You plan to eventually eliminate Social Security, Medicare, and other social services. How long would that take? What would the transition process be like?

Since generations of Americans have been raised to depend on government entitlements I recognize the need to move in responsible steps and speed. We currently spend nearly $1 trillion a year overseas. I would cut that substantially and apply the hundreds of billions of dollars of savings to fund Social Security and Medicare while at the same introducing market-based solutions as options for younger people. I would also never, and have never, raided the Social Security trust fund. That money belongs to the American people and should never be used as a slush fund for politicians pet spending projects.

If you abolish the Department of Education, does that mean there would be no taxpayer funded schools at all, on all levels? What if some parents are not able to pay and no charity is available to them?

Education policy should be set by parents working with state and local governments, not bureaucrats in Washington. Abolishing the Department of Education would eliminate only the federal role in taxpayer funding, which is a small percentage of total education funding; moreover, the conflicting federal strings on this funding often outweigh the benefits to the education of our children. My efforts to reduce the cost of government would create an environment where more people could afford the education of their choice and Americans would be better able to help others in need.

A person is bleeding. He comes to a hospital. He has no insurance and no money. There is no charity available. Can he be turned away?

While this is clearly not a federal issue, professional oaths, missions of the hospitals, etc., would prohibit an injured patient bleeding from being turned away. In my own medical practice I routinely gave free or discounted care to patients less able to pay.

Should abortion be a state issue? Wouldn't that make abortion essentially legal everywhere since pregnant women in a pro-life state could just go to a neighboring pro-choice state for an abortion and come back?

The constitution does not authorize the federal government regulate abortion. Murder is illegal all over the country with variations across the states regarding manslaughter versus murder and its degrees. Similarly, abortion should be decided at the state level.

What would you do about the environment, especially on public lands? Would you sell off Yellowstone and other national parks to the highest bidder, even if it meant the land would be drilled for oil?

This is a multi-faceted question. As a medical doctor, I took an oath to do no harm. Similarly, I have worked with the Green Scissors coalition to eliminate harmful government spending and regularly rate or near the top of Congressmen on their scorecard. Obviously, I would never to go war over oil. Also, I would end special interest favors and subsidies that harm the environment; I have opposed programs to subsidize development in environmentally fragile areas with taxpayer-subsidized flood insurance, etc. One of the lessons of Katrina is that oil exploration and development have progressed in ways that environmental concerns are mitigated even under severe natural disasters.

Would you start deporting the 7 to 20 million illegal aliens in America today? And what would you do to prevent them from just coming back?

Since we get more of what we subsidize and less of what we tax, we are reaping today the effects of our immigration policy that encourages illegal immigration. The incentives of birthright citizenship and federally mandated education, medical care and welfare assistance for illegals are powerful incentives for people to come here illegally. While identifying and deporting all of the so many millions of people here illegally today (many of whom came legally and overstayed their welcome) would be nearly impossible, we should enforce the law. We should also tighten citizenship requirements, reject amnesty and end welfare-state benefits for those here illegally.

Everybody talks about freedom, peace, smaller government, fiscal responsibility and so on. The Republican Party traditionally talks about it and when people vote for them, as with the Contract with America, or Ronald Reagan, they do practically nothing of what they promised. Once we vote for them, the size of government increases and the debt increases. Why should we believe you now? Can you offer something more than just promises?

Excellent question: As a ten-term Congressman active in public life for three decades, my record has been one of consistency. I say what I mean and mean what I say even if I'm the only correct vote in the congress.

Originally published on June 20, 2007

INTERVIEW WITH MIKE GRAVEL

Democratic presidential candidate Senator Mike Gravel is literally none of the above. He stopped being a senator in 1981. He stopped being a Democrat last week when he switched to the Libertarian Party to seek its nomination. And he stopped being a traditional, power-hungry presidential candidate as of this interview when he declared that even if he won, he would resign as president if his National Initiative legislation was not passed.

But one thing he has never stopped being is outspoken. In 1971, his five-month-long, one-man filibuster helped end the draft. He brought the Pentagon Papers, a top-secret 7,000-page report detailing how our government misled us into the Vietnam War, into the public record by reading them from the floor of the senate. This election cycle, his animated participation in the Democratic debates and his anti-war, anti-tax stance (he'd get out of Iraq within 120 days and replace all federal taxes with the Fair Tax, a national retail sales tax) got him more web traffic than those of the Democratic front-runners, at least for one month, and his iconoclastic and mildly hypnotic YouTube commercial of him silently staring into the camera for two minutes has been viewed more than half a million times.

Sen. Gravel is an interesting and colorful man and our conversation was twice as long as you see here. Each cut word was painful and unfortunately makes the interview appear more abrupt than it really was. What's missing? Sen. Gravel's thoughts on the FDA (should be essentially abolished), Dr. Kevorkian (his jailing was terrible and he'd endorse his recent run for Congress if he also ran as a Libertarian), DNC chairman Howard Dean (who once called him an "asshole" over the mic), war (over the past century, only WWII and Afghanistan have been justified), lots more about the National Initiative (including how it has worked in practice in Switzerland), Barack Obama (who doesn't tell the truth about taking money from lobbyists), and more.

Is Sen. Gravel a Libertarian? That's for you to decide.

Phil Maymin: A lot of libertarians feel that the U.S. should not really be involved with the UN that much, that it takes away American sovereignty to give up certain rights to the UN. How do you feel about that?

Mike Gravel: There's two levels of sovereignty. There's the level of sovereignty of the group and the level of sovereignty of the individual. You have given up your sovereignty to your local government, your state government, and your federal government. Now your federal government is acting in your behalf to go start wars and kill people and to use the United Nations for whatever it wants to do, screwing around in the world. Okay?

Now, if you really wanted to recognize that we do need some kind of global governance, because we don't control the corporations that are controlling our lives right now. They're out there in no-man's-land, doing what they want to do. So what we need to do is have some level of global governance. Now, is that going to rely upon the nation-state? Or is it going to rely upon you with your sovereignty?

Now, if we had the National Initiative in place where you can exercise your sovereignty at the local level, the state level, and the federal level, and maybe the global level, where it's dependent upon you directly, and not dependent upon the federal government. You see the difference I'm drawing?

Maymin: I understand what you're saying. You're adding an extra layer on top of the federal layer of government.

Gravel: But I'm having it dependent upon you, not the Congress or the government.

Maymin: But the history over the past 50 years has been ethnic groups trying to create their own countries so they can govern themselves. If we go into "everybody votes across the world on what to do with America's money," that's not fair.

Gravel: Wait a sec. They're not voting on what to do with America's money. They're doing that right now with the UN.

Maymin: Well, that's what I mean.

Gravel: We pay our dues. But wait a second. Explain to me how we're ever going to have peace in the world when everybody can have armies and go to war.

Maymin: I think that's the only way we will have peace is if everybody has armies.

Gravel: Oh! Wait a second, wait a second. That's what we've been having since the beginning of civilization.

Maymin: No, we've had people trying to take away other people's armies. We've had America interfering with other people's business. An army is for defense, it's not an offensive army, where you go marching to create an empire. That's where the trouble comes. It's like with a gun.

Gravel: Well, how do you stop that? How do you stop that?

Maymin: How do you stop evil?

Gravel: No, how do you stop people from going around creating empires?

Maymin: Well, if it's my country on my tax dollars trying to go around, then I have a right to stop it and a duty to stop it.

Gravel: Tell me how you're doing it because you're not doing a good job at it right now.

Maymin: Right, but the problem is that the federal government is too powerful. Adding an extra layer of government...

Gravel: How do you stop that?

Maymin: ...is the wrong solution. You take away power from the federal government.

Gravel: Here, I know the problem, you know the problem. What's the solution?

Maymin: What's the solution? You know, elect a Libertarian President. Elect a Libertarian Congress.

Gravel: Oh really? Hey, a Libertarian President can't do shit.

Maymin: Well, no, first of all, the wars and foreign policy...

Gravel: Wait a sec, here, I'm a Libertarian. Make me president, I can't do a goddamn thing more than what anybody else can do. Now if the American people can make laws then I can do something.

Maymin: If you're the president, why can't you just pull all the troops back from all bases overseas and bring them all home?

Gravel: Hey, don't you know how the Congress works?

Maymin: But you're in charge of the army.

Gravel: Who's in the Congress? What's the Congress gonna do? It's gonna be made up of Democrats and Republicans?

Maymin: They can do whatever. They can pass whatever laws they want, at the end of the day it's your decision where to send the troops. You can always bring them home.

Gravel: You can only do what they appropriate money for. Please. Regardless of whether it's McCain or Hillary or Obama, they're all going to be war-making and drawing us into wars.

So if I were president, sure I could withdraw the troops, but then it won't be any significant change until the people can make laws.

It's only with the people—see, what I would do, how I could end the military-industrial complex, is I would ask the people as lawmakers to give me the line-item veto and I would sit in the Oval Office with the military appropriations legislation and I would go through it like a dose of salts. That's how I'd do it. That's simple. But it's the people who have given me the power to do it. Without that, I can't do a thing.

Maymin: Okay.

Gravel: The military-industrial complex owns the country. They own us, right now. Lock, stock, and barrel, and they've militarized our culture, and they own the media. They own everything. You think you can elect somebody president on that score?

Here, I'm trying by becoming a Libertarian to get across the message and it's a Libertarian message. Now I don't know if the Libertarians, if you as a Libertarian will understand that you got all these views on Libertarianism but the most important thing about Libertarianism is to empower the people to have liberty. And you can only have liberty and freedom if you can make laws.

Maymin: Let me try to challenge that, if I may. The point of liberty and libertarianism is so you can live your life the way you want to so long as you don't harm other people, right? That's the basic idea. So to the extent you have more of an ability to pass laws, that's really giving you power not over yourself but over your fellow Americans. And that's not liberty. That's in some at least theoretical sense taking away liberty overall.

Gravel: No! No. Because you see you're not alone on the planet. You're part of a society. And so you as an individual are alone, you want your liberty, so fine, you can go be Jeremiah Johnson, go live in the forest and eat twigs. But when you come into society you have to have rules for the functioning of society. And those rules are determined, they're called laws. And Solon in 595 BC brought out this concept of laws. And so now the key is laws. And so if you really want to enjoy your liberty as part of a collective society, you have to become a lawmaker. Cicero, more than two thousand years, defined freedom. Now freedom is the exercise of liberty. Do you understand that concept?

So, now, to have freedom you must participate in power. In a democracy, power is the central part of government, which is lawmaking. So if you want to have freedom, you must become a lawmaker. If you're not part of making laws, you're not part of power. And so therefore you're stuck as an individual, wanting to be free and have liberty, but all you can do is obey the goddamn laws some other people pass for you. Are you beginning to understand that?

Maymin: No, I understand what you're saying.

Gravel: No, you're not understanding what I'm saying because you think you can have your libertarian liberty without being part of the power structure of making laws.

Maymin: Well, I think this definition of the word "power" is being used in two different senses. I should have power over myself. So for example, my money, I earned it from somebody, who should decide...

Gravel: Of course, you have the power over that. That's a given. It's your money.

Maymin: So I should be able to decide what to do with my money, right?

Gravel: Of course. But now you live in a society that has roads and so you must contribute some portion of your money to pay for the roads you're going to drive on.

Maymin: Right, so that's where we disagree. I don't think everybody on earth should be deciding what to do with my money.

Gravel: Well then don't drive on the roads! Go back into the wilderness.

Maymin: Yeah, that's fine, maybe roads should not be publicly funded or maybe they should be locally funded.

Gravel: Well, wait a second, who's local? If I go into your town and drive on your roads and enjoy the benefit of that, then why should you pay for my benefit?

Maymin: Oh, I may well install a toll.

Gravel: Well, that's fine. We do that. I got an EZ Pass.

Maymin: Right. The problem is things like welfare, or Social Security, or education.

Gravel: But you recognize that in a complex society, whether it's local or global, we need laws. And what I'm trying to point out to you is that at the global level we have anarchy. And you know who gets screwed when you got anarchy, is the individual loses liberty. That's what happens. And the people who have military might, profit. And that's what's going on in the world today.

Maymin: What about things like education and health care? There doesn't seem to be any Constitutional authority for the federal government to provide those services.

Gravel: Well, how are you going to get people educated then?

Maymin: There may be lots of problems in the world, one of which may be education, but if it's not authorized, it's not authorized.

Gravel: Let's pose the question. We're both Libertarians. How are we going to get the people educated so that they can be good Libertarians?

Maymin: How are you going to educate him? Are you going to take my money to educate him?

Gravel: I don't know who, I don't know.

Maymin: Well, if you want to take my money, then you have to have some authority to do so.

Gravel: Well, fine. Then you want everybody dumb? Uneducated?

Maymin: I want everybody free.

Gravel: Freedom involves having knowledge, doesn't it?

Maymin: No. No. Freedom involves being free from oppression, not having other people take your money or your time or your abilities. Not being forced to sit in a school that looks just like a jail for 12-13 years of your life, right? That's not freedom.

Gravel: No, that's stupid education.

Maymin: Yes.

Gravel: So if you're not smart enough to get in there and help design a decent education system, then you're going to get this dumb education system that you refuse to get involved with in designing.

Maymin: But I can design a private education system.

Gravel: Well, fine. Then do that.

Maymin: Fine, but then everybody is involved voluntarily. There's no use of force.

Gravel: Well, fine. Then we'll all do things voluntarily.

Maymin: Okay.

Gravel: Well, good. Then fine. We won't build any roads unless you want to pave it. We'll have anarchy. Everything's going to be voluntary.

Maymin: Wait, why is it anarchy? If it's voluntary...

Gravel: It is anarchy. It is anarchy. Because why should I turn around and pay for it when I can live off of you?

Maymin: Right, I'm not going to force you to pay for it if you don't want to...

Gravel: That's fine, I'll just suck off of you. Why the hell should I lift a finger?

Maymin: No, you don't have to. I mean, people give to charities...

Gravel: You're right I don't have to, and I won't! I'll just suck off of you. I'll stand on a corner and beg off of you when you walk by.

Maymin: You're welcome to do that but I am under no obligation to give money on the corner.

Gravel: Of course you don't have to give. Of course you don't have to give. So what will happen is if you don't give and I get hungry enough I'll take a goddamn knife and I'll take it from you.

Maymin: Well, that's the purpose of government. That's where the difference between anarchy and libertarian government comes into play, because then we have a justice system...

Gravel: Tell me about libertarian government. You got any in the world?

Maymin: Well, I mean, it's an ideal, though America used to be fairly libertarian...

Gravel: Well, wait a sec. One of the things of life is, you know, you can design all these kinds of perfect theories that's really down to practicalities don't make any sense.

Maymin: What doesn't make sense about going back to basically the way things were before we had a Department of Education or a Department of Energy?

Gravel: Oh, you want to roll the clock back?

Maymin: I want to roll freedom forward.

Gravel: Is that really what you're advocating? Before, we had no education in this country?

Maymin: Wait, are you talking about public or private education?

Gravel: I'm talking about, there was no education. I don't give a shit whether it's public or private. When we had no education, is that what you want?

Maymin: I don't remember a time when we had no education. I know a time when we had no public education. Things were certainly better in terms of people being better educated.

Gravel: Oh, come on. Please... Here, you can take your libertarianism to extreme and it's not libertarianism. It truly isn't. It truly isn't. It becomes marginally unfunctional.

Maymin: How would you define libertarianism?

Gravel: I'd define libertarianism having liberty and freedom in a complex society that recognizes the freedom of others...

And that means you gotta have laws. And since you gotta have laws, then I want to be party to making the laws. That's the only protection I have is to be party to making the laws. And that means that I want the people to make the laws to protect themselves. That's why I say that the National Initiative is more libertarian than anything anybody in the Libertarian Party has ever thought of.

Maymin: To the extent that the National Initiative does not pass, and you are the president, then what do you do?

Gravel: What would I do? I would bully the people to vote to put it in place and if they don't put it in place, I wouldn't stay as president.

What the hell am I gonna do? Just enjoy the perks of the White House and sit with the Congress and fight over nothing? Oh sure, I'd end the war. But they would win. They've won in the past. It's a silly game. It's an ego trip at that point, and I don't want it. At my age, what do I need that for?

Maymin: You don't think you could do a lot of good as president even without the National Initiative?

Gravel: What's a lot of good? My God.

Maymin: You know, you could end the war on drugs...

Gravel: Listen, I was in elective office for 16 years. I ended the draft. I stopped the nuclear testing in the north Pacific. I released the Pentagon Papers. Tell me about all the good I did when we now went back into Iraq and we're still killing people.

Maymin: Well, you did good.

Gravel: I know I've done good but it didn't do enough. It's all forgotten. We're worse off today than when I was in office. We're worse off today...

I don't have any magic answers. I have the same conclusions that you have. But I'm not arrogant enough to think that, boy, this is what's got to be done. I've made too many laws in my life where I saw that they have unintended consequences.

Here, I'll give you an unintended consequence. I ended the draft. We've got over a hundred thousand mercenaries in Iraq today. That's an unintended consequence of my ending the draft.

So it's tough to really pat yourself on the back saying how great you are when you see this kind of crap happen as a result of what you've done. Yet I'm proud of what I've done there, but still...

Maymin: I understand. I think what you're saying is you're looking for one big thing you can do, right? That would do a lot of good for a long period of time, and the National Initiative is...

Gravel: That's right. I'll be long gone... I want to give the Libertarians a tool that then will help them bring about what Libertarian is really all about. And that is for the people to be free. And how do you become free, is as Cicero said, you participate in power. If you can't participate in power, you cannot be free...

And I hear what you're saying about education. I got the same views. Like I say, I can say it with a clear conscience: fire all the damn school boards!

We've fractured our educational system. I see the countries that are succeeding in education flies right in the face of your views on libertarianism: Finland, Sweden, Spain—they all have national standards and they all fund education for the student's entire life, all the way up to the Ph.D.

Maymin: They also have school choice, which we don't have.

Gravel: They do?

Maymin: I think a lot of them do. They have a voucher program and so there's some...

Gravel: Oh, well, no, the voucher program, that's it for me. That's for sure. That's a given. That's a given.

Maymin: Then you have at least some competition so you go back to at least a little bit of...

Gravel: That's a given. I wouldn't even argue that point. I assume that. When I talk about getting rid of the damn unions, I'm talking about that.

The voucher. And see, the voucher, you could pay your mother to teach you full time, if she's qualified. And as long as you could pass some tests.

Here, I would pay people—like if you got a sick mother, rather than have you go get on welfare or Medicare, Medicaid, whatever, if you're going to stay home and take care of your parents, you should be able to—if we're going to pay other people to do that, why not pay you to do it, rather than you go to work, and then pay your taxes, and then we have your taxes pay somebody else to do it. Here again, it's common sense, that if we had a lot of that, and people have this creativity.

If we would just get the government out of the way.

Maymin: Yeah.

Gravel: But people will do that. We talk of, you want less government? You will never, never get less government until you put the people in power. You see whenever something goes wrong what does a politician think of? First, "Oh, I got a solution."

Listen to Obama talk. Goddamn, every time he opens his mouth he's spending another hundred bucks on you. [Laughing] And Hillary the same. And if you can read the code, so is McCain. But you gotta be able to read the code. That's the way politicians think. You know why they think that way? They want you to love 'em. "Vote for me, I'm going to do things for you."

But that's not the way the people think. The people look at the problem and they say, "Hmm. Now maybe if I leave it alone, it'll go away." [Laughing.] You know something? It may go away! Nine times out of ten, it will. That's the reason the Hippocratic oath is very interesting. It says, "First, do no harm." And that's what politicians do not understand.

Maymin: If you had to vote for one of the other three guys, who would you vote for?

Gravel: I wouldn't. Because they're terrible...I'd vote for myself.

Obama is not good. Obama, there's a very really difficult situation. When you raise people's expectations, and you can't deliver, you really, really do a lot of damage. Hillary will do less damage, because she's not raising expectations.

Maymin: What an interesting way of looking at it. Wow.

Gravel: What's more damage? If I raise your expectations, and I don't deliver, I make a cynic out of you. And that's the worst thing you can do to a population is to make them a bunch of cynics. Then they have no hope. And that's what Obama's doing. He can't deliver on anything he's talking about. And plus he doesn't tell the truth either.

Maymin: I guess that's another nice thing about the National Initiative, right? There's no natural way for parties to form.

Gravel: That's right—you've just put your finger on something! You see, here, if the Libertarians became a full-fledged party like the Democratic Party, they will act just like the Democratic Party (laughing). Power corrupts.

Maymin: That's the danger.

Gravel: But if the Libertarian Party gets a President and enacts the National Initiative, you don't need the parties. The people will be the disciplinarians. It may cause the disappearance of the parties. I don't know.

What's going to be the unintended consequence of empowering the people? I don't know. But one of the things, possible, it could do away with the parties, which is what the founding fathers feared the most, which was the parties.

What we're just articulating is the first time I've ever articulated that. I never thought of it.

Originally published on April 3, 2008

INTERVIEW WITH RICHARD THALER

Richard Thaler is the father of the behavioral economics movement, the Director of the Center for Decision Research at the University of Chicago, and the co-author of *Nudge*, a new book promoting a political "third way" called libertarian paternalism. An article in last month's *New Republic* described him as the "intellectual guru" behind Barack Obama, though when I asked him what position he would like in an Obama administration, he said he wouldn't be interested (except perhaps as the spouse to the ambassador to St. Barts), though he'd be willing to be the Secretary of Nudging.

He was also my professor, dissertation adviser, and mentor over the past decade or so as I was a Ph.D. student in Finance at the University of Chicago's Graduate School of Business. (I finally graduated last year.) He is also one of the most remarkable people I have ever met.

I am a hard man to sway. I came to the University of Chicago after being a trader at Long-Term Capital Management in the years surrounding and including the infamous incident of 1998. I had heard about behavioral economics and its use of psychology in finance and I was pretty sure it was rubbish. But, in one of the best open-minded decisions I ever made, I took Prof. Thaler's course my first semester there. He was incredibly persuasive. It literally changed my life. Looked at in the new light, the purely rational approach was really just a subset of the behavioral approach.

Would the same thing happen with his book? Would I shed my purely libertarian beliefs as easily and as permanently as I shed my purely rational ones? After all, rationality and libertarianism often travel together (c.f. Ayn Rand). See for yourself below, though I will give you a hint: libertarianism is *not* a subset of libertarian paternalism.

Nudge itself can serve as a fascinating apolitical read, for example, as a self-help book, or as a way for a company to benefit its employees through subtle cues to help them choose what would be better for them anyway, if they had the time and energy. Things like savings decisions or picking lunch: choice is preserved for those who want low savings or fatty fries, but the defaults are higher savings and healthy salads.

But it is the political realm that makes it most controversial, at least to me. As a new political movement, it's not even clear what the official stance is on many issues. How does a libertarian paternalist stack up against the standard political groups? To answer, I put Prof. Thaler through the World's Shortest Political Quiz, the first time libertarian paternalism has been placed on the political map. The quiz is composed of five questions about personal issues and five about economic issues and you can either choose agree, maybe, or disagree. See the results in the sidebar. You can take the quiz yourself at theadvocates.org/quiz to see where you fall.

Where did Prof. Thaler think he would end up? "I think I'm somewhere to the right of Ron Paul." He exclaimed a delighted "Yes!" when he found out he was labeled as a libertarian, but then he corrected the quiz results. "But," he said. "I'm a libertarian paternalist."

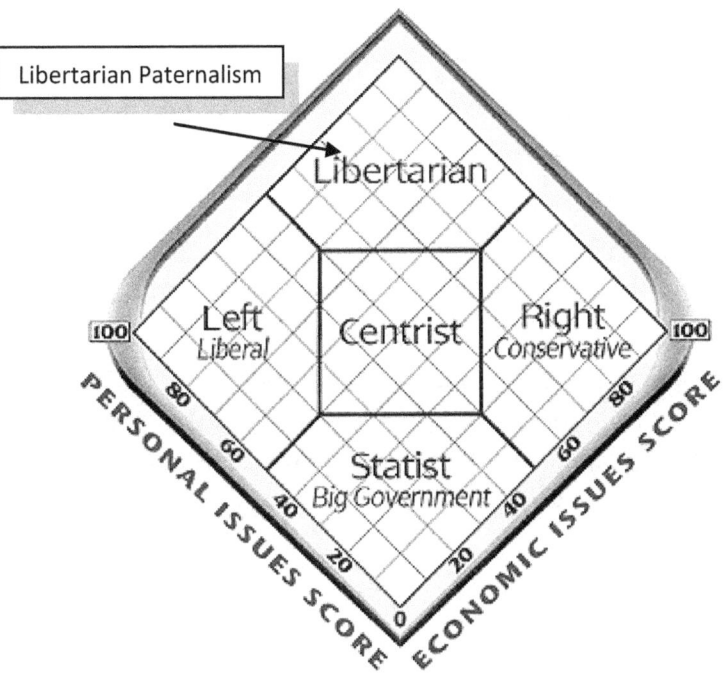

PERSONAL ISSUES	
Government should not censor speech, press, media or Internet.	Agree
Military service should be voluntary. There should be no draft.	Agree
There should be no laws regarding sex for consenting adults.	Agree
Repeal laws prohibiting adult possession and use of drugs.	Agree
There should be no National ID card.	Maybe

ECONOMIC ISSUES	
End "corporate welfare." No government handouts to business.	Agree
End government barriers to international free trade.	Agree
Let people control their own retirement; privatize Social Security.	Maybe
Replace government welfare with private charity.	Maybe
Cut taxes and government spending by 50% or more.	Maybe

Maymin: You say you want to bridge the gap between Democrats and Republicans, but you have two elephants on your cover and no donkey.

Thaler: <Laughter>

Maymin: What's up?

Thaler: Yeah, well we couldn't find a picture of a donkey nudging so we went with the elephants. It's funny we did get some complaints from Democratic friends saying, "Why did you put a picture of elephants on the cover?" But we think that the image of the mother elephant nudging the baby sort of captures what the book is about, because the baby's free to go wherever she wants.

Maymin: I'll tell you why libertarians have a problem, and it's that the word "liberal" used to mean someone who is for freedom and liberty.

Thaler: Right.

Maymin: But then FDR started calling himself a liberal. The meaning changed and us freedom loving Americans were forced to contrive this new word, libertarian. And it feels like you have kind of taken that word away from us too.

Thaler: Right, but we're using it as an adjective. So, it's not like we're calling ourselves libertarians. We're calling ourselves libertarian paternalists. And so it's meant to be a modifier. So, if I say, I'm serving you Japanese-French food, I'm not claiming to serve you Japanese food.

Maymin: Okay, but if you say you're serving non-food food, then it gets confusing. So if libertarian is modifying paternalism, how can it be libertarian in any meaningful sense?

Thaler: Well, probably because by adding the adjective to the word paternalism we're eliminating the part of paternalism that you most strongly object to. So, in spite of the fact that you're a libertarian, you're a nice guy. And, you know, I've never seen you, like, push old ladies down in the street or, you know, you don't think that we should make poor people poorer. So, I think helping people make better decisions is something that is unobjectionable, and that's all we mean by paternalistic.

But when libertarians use the word paternalism, there is a sense in which libertarian paternalism is an oxymoron. And, of course, we chose the phrase precisely because it seems to be contradictory and controversial. If we knew enough to write this book and didn't pick a controversial word to describe it, we should bury our heads in the sand. So, it's an intentional oxymoron, or at least an ironic phrase.

And the way we get it, I don't think that it's an oxymoron or misleading because by paternalism, libertarians mean forcing people to do something, and of course, then there can't be libertarian paternalism.

But what we think is, it's about things like choosing the right default and, as you know, our argument is, well, you've got to pick one, there has to be a default, why not pick the one that you think is the better one by some criteria.

Maymin: So, of the defaults in, say, Medicare prescription plans - you make an excellent case that there should be a better way of picking defaults than randomness or other things, but at the end of the day, Medicare itself is paternalistic. It's forcing people who don't want to be in the program to pay for other people's benefits.

Thaler: That's right, but, you see, this is why I think libertarians have less influence than they should. So let me really piss you and your readers off by scolding you.

Maymin: Please.

Thaler: Here's what I mean by that. We have the prescription drug program. It was passed by a Republican President and a Republican dominated Congress. And in our book, we have nothing to say about whether having such a program was a good or bad idea. We're agnostic about that. What we say is if you're going to have such a program, then how should you do it?

So, is it a good idea to maximize the number of choices? Now, some people take it as an article of religious faith that the more choices you have the better, and I think that should be an empirical question. Are people, in fact, better off when they choose from fifty plans than from ten plans? Right? That's a study-able question. And as you know, we studied the Swedish Social Security System, where they had 456 options. I think it's safe to say that 456 is more than the optimal number of choices.

So, you know, back to my libertarian bashing, the partial privatization of Social Security, I think libertarians should applaud, but they might just say, "Well, we shouldn't have Social Security at all," but, that just leaves them out of the discussion. And renders them irrelevant. And what we're trying to do is say, well, can we utilize some libertarian principles and get right into the middle of the debate. So, libertarians, I think, are unfairly viewed as, you know, somewhere to the right of Donald Rumsfeld. And, as we know, this administration has probably been the least libertarian administration in the history of the country.

And, so, the Republicans have no claim, whatsoever, to libertarian values. So, I think what we're trying to offer libertarians in this book is a way to stop being irrelevant and start being relevant. And, you know, sure you might rather have no prescription drug program and no Medicare, but that's not where we are right now.

And it's a question of what sort of Medicare program are we going to have, and what sort of Social Security are we going to have, and what sort of regulation are we going to have for mortgages? Saying the government should just get out is just making yourself irrelevant.

Boy, that was unexpected.

Maymin: <Laughter> Why?

Thaler: Well, I mean, I just hadn't ever given that speech before.

Maymin: <Laughter> It actually taps into something deep that's happening in the Libertarian Party now. In the last election cycle, they threw away this pure, wonderful, idealistic platform and made it a pragmatic thing of, you know, we should have school choice as opposed to no Department of Education, but that sort of thing.

Thaler: Right, right, right. That's exactly what I'm saying. And, you know, it's funny, I was at a fundraiser with Obama...no it wasn't, that's not right. It wasn't a fundraiser for Obama, it was a fundraiser for some woman who was running for Congress, but it was organized by a bunch of rich liberals who had supported Obama. And one of them was saying, "You know, we were all supporters of Barack from a long time, but then he went to Washington, and he became pragmatic!" And it was like they were saying "Oh, that's so terrible." And, you know, I was ready to kill them.

Maymin: <Laughter>

Thaler: Because it's that sort of thinking that gets you more of George Bush. So I think that a pragmatic libertarian candidate, that's an appealing idea, and we've given them the platform.

Maymin: Actually, in a recent interview, your co-author, Cass Sunstein, says you are a libertarian, in the sense that you really don't like government mandates and stuff. Is that true?

Thaler: You mean me personally?

Maymin: You personally.

Thaler: Well, I don't think that I'm a capital "L" libertarian. But, I mean, the history of this phrase is that I was presenting a paper here at the University of Chicago on the "Save More Tomorrow" Program, and a guy in the Economics Department was my discussant and he accused me of being a paternalist. Which as you know is the biggest insult that you can accuse anybody of being at the University of Chicago. And I said, "Well, I guess, but there's no coercion here, so, maybe you should call me a libertarian paternalist." That's where it started. And, I don't think a libertarian can have any objection to "Save More Tomorrow."

Maymin: When it's within a company.

Thaler: When it's within a company.

Maymin: Right, but that's -

Thaler: Now, so let's get the government involved. So, there was the Pension Protection Act, and what it did is it nudged companies in the following way: It said, "If you offer a match, and Save More Tomorrow, and automatic enrollment, then we give you a free pass on the non-discrimination rules."

So, it didn't say anybody had to do it. It just said, "We're going to make your life a little easier over here if you do this."

I don't know how much you know about them, the non-discrimination rules just say that you're not allowed to give more than "X" percent of the benefits to the highest paid workers. And in the 401k, since there's a dollar max, then the only way you can be in violation of those rules is if you don't get the low paid workers to join. Right? There's no way to give the CEO a million dollar pension contribution.

So, we do accomplish that goal because if you automatically enroll and automatically escalate, then the poor will save enough to get the company into compliance, and they just don't have to bother to prove it. So, I think that's pretty admirable libertarian paternalism legislation. Because it's pushing a libertarian paternalism idea and it's just nudging it.

Maymin: What about more complicated things, like, what about drugs, whether it's marijuana or FDA drugs? What would be the libertarian paternalistic approach to that?

Thaler: Yeah, I mean, we didn't write about those things. I think both of us tend to think that prohibition was a fiasco and that we should have learned our lessons and, you know, it's pretty clear, that marijuana should be decriminalized. Now how far do you push that, I don't know. You know, if there's some drug that has a 90% chance to kill you, I don't know what the libertarian position is on that.

Maymin: You own your body.

Thaler: Have I ever given you my sunlamp example?

Maymin: Sunlamp, no, I don't think so.

Thaler: Sunlamps, I don't know if they're really popular any more, but they certainly used to be popular. You turn it on, and you close your eyes, and you stay under it for a few minutes to get a tan. Now, closing your eyes and having warm temperature is very likely to produce sleep.

So lots of people burned themselves. Now, so, sunlamps should be equipped with a timer switch. Now, suppose that you can equip a sunlamp with a timer switch for a quarter.

I think that's probably a good idea, because, now that's not libertarian. That's just like -

Maymin: You mean as a law or as a -

Thaler: As a law. Now, there we're going to get down slippery slopes, but if you say, "All right, I'm God, do I think that's a good law or a bad law?" I think that's a good law.

Maymin: On the basis of what, how do you decide what's a good law and what's a bad law?

Thaler: Well, that's what I'm explaining.

Maymin: Okay.

Thaler: If the probability of error is very high and the cost you impose on people is very low, then I think there's a case to be made. And so, like there's this paper on what they call Asymmetric Paternalism. And that's sort of their principle. That you want to help people, but while imposing the fewest costs on the sophisticated people. So you're making everybody pay a quarter and some people would always bring their kitchen timer. But of course we know even the people who would usually do that would occasionally forget their kitchen timer and would occasionally burn themselves.

Maymin: Right. So it's a cost benefit analysis, basically.

Thaler: It's a cost benefit analysis, right. I can see that you would have trouble with that.

Maymin: Well, I would say that if it's a just law, then it's a good law. You can't make laws that help plunder; you can't initiate force against other people. That's what makes a bad law. It's a moral thing.

Thaler: Right, right, but you know, a $0.25 switch is not plunder.

Maymin: But you're initiating force. I mean, if you mug somebody for a quarter, should you not be prosecuted?

Thaler: No, but you're imposing costs of more than a quarter.

Maymin: Well, who's to decide what the costs are? That's the attraction of libertarianism is that it's a moral stance.

Thaler: So these are precisely the issues that we duck in this book. Because, we've decided to write a whole book on Libertarian Paternalism, and then as you know, in the Objections chapter we say, "Well, we can be criticized from the left and the right." And the people on the left want to say, "Well, shouldn't we have some pure paternalism?" And so my answer to them is, "Well, if you want my personal opinion, I think the sunlamp rule, I would personally be in favor of that." But, we're writing a book where we have a bright line and we're going to stick to that.

Maymin: Okay, let's talk about the mortgage stuff.

Thaler: Yeah, I think this is our best idea.

Maymin: Okay, so a few days ago, in the Boston Globe, you described a proposal. You want to give aid, as you say, to those who were bamboozled.

Thaler: Yeah.

Maymin: But why should I pay for that, if I didn't bamboozle anybody?

Thaler: I mean, this is actually beyond the scope of our book, so we're just talking about... this is like what we were talking about at the beginning. There's going to be aid. You know, everybody in Congress is falling all over themselves to try and help. And, you know, I think you can make the argument about Bear Stearns, or your former employer [Long-Term Capital Management].

Maymin: <Laughter> That was a private bail-out!

Thaler: <Laughter> That's right. This one was *mostly* private, but the government got involved in both cases. And you can say there are externalities. You know, the Bear Stearns shareholders certainly are not coming out whole any more than the LTCM partners did.

Maymin: This is the problem with pragmatic libertarianism: the fear of legitimizing the current state of affairs. You say that stabilizing the real estate market is a legitimate government goal. But what makes it legitimate?

Thaler: Well, I mean, in the same sense of stabilizing, exactly the same argument you can make for making sure that Bear

Stearns doesn't fail because what would that do to financial markets if all of a sudden there was this huge counterparty risk.

Maymin: So you're basically in favor of the Bear Stearns bail-out too?

Thaler: Again, I don't have a professional opinion about that. I would say that, this is no worse than that. That you can make an argument that there is some social good that came about because of that. And essentially that by irresponsible risk management, Bear Stearns was going to impose huge costs on lots of people, and what the Fed did was greatly reduce those costs and give some benefit to Bear Stearns, but not much.

Maymin: Okay, so let's talk about the electronic stuff. Basically, if I understand it, you want to, essentially, augment the Truth in Lending Act to force mortgage brokers and others to provide an electronic file and a standardized form that lists every feature to ease comparison across providers. Right?

Thaler: Right.

Maymin: Now, will one of the columns in the standardized form be something like a comment or footnote section?

Thaler: All of the footnotes will be in there.

Maymin: Okay, so, they get a text area where they can say something that doesn't quite fit into something.

Thaler: No.

Maymin: No? So there would be no further innovation in mortgages?

Thaler: You'd have to apply. So, we haven't written at length about how we imagine this working, but let's talk about, say, cell phone plans, because it's a little easier to understand. So, suppose somebody comes up with the iPhone and it allows you to download songs, which didn't exist before, so what we would imagine is that there would be a process whereby a cell phone provider would say, we want a new category, and we just want it added to the list of things that you can charge for. And for such applications, the presumption is that they would be approved.

Maymin: So people have gone from pleasing the customer to pleasing governmental officials?

Thaler: No, they just have to announce.

Maymin: What do you mean announce? If I just put it on my website that this is the new plan, is that enough?

Thaler: No, you would have to, and I don't know exactly how this process should work, but they would have to agree, you'd have to get permission to have this new way of charging.

Maymin: But isn't that terrible? I mean, before, if I want to offer you, personally, if I have some benefit to offer you, that's it, but now, instead of just me and you agreeing, we have to involve a third party who has his own issues.

Thaler: Um.

Maymin: Isn't that the death of contracts? Imagine if this had happened before, you know, thirty years ago or something, when every, all mortgages were just 30-year fixed; we would have never had variable rate mortgages.

Thaler: No, that's exactly wrong.

Maymin: Okay, why?

Thaler: Because the presumption will be that *any* kind of new innovation will be approved.

Maymin: But approved by whom?

Thaler: By... because the regulator is not saying what you can do and not do, all the regulator is doing is providing a way to make comparisons. So, if you want to have a new kind of variable rate, or interest only mortgage, or any other kind of exotica, the only thing you would be required to do is explain to the regulator how this is going to work, so they can incorporate it into their spreadsheets. That's all.

Maymin: So we become a country where we have to ask permission to innovate.

Thaler: No, we just have to report it. That's all. I think you're making the permission part... so look, for years, credit card companies were secretly charging people 3% on their foreign transactions and not revealing it. Or if it was revealed, it was deep in some fine print. So, I don't think they used to do that, they got this clever idea to do it, and they didn't tell anybody about it. So, under our régime, they would have to announce it and not deep in the fine print. They'd have to announce it to a regulator because the regulator would have to write another line of code to include that in the electronic disclosure. I don't think that is so bad.

[Here we went through the ten-question political quiz.]

Maymin: Have you spoken to political groups?

Thaler: We both spoke at AEI [the neoconservative think tank] last week. And that went very well. I think our message appeals pretty much across the board. Most vehement objections are from libertarians and I think most of those come from people who haven't read the book.

Maymin: Not all.

Thaler: <Laughter> I know.

Maymin: <Laughter>

Thaler: But I like you anyway.

Originally published on May 6, 2008

www.ingramcontent.com/pod-product-compliance
Lightning Source LLC
Chambersburg PA
CBHW060620290526
45793CB00001B/93